STRIPER HOT SPOTS

MIDDLE ATLANTIC

T0119441

STRIPER HOT SPOTS

MIDDLE ATLANTIC

FRANK DAIGNAULT

BURFORD BOOKS

Printed in the United States of America.

10 9 8 7 6 5 4 3 2 1

Library of Congress Cataloging-in-Publication data is on file with the Library of Congress.

Manufactured in the United States of America

CONTENTS

New Jersey

New York

Connecticut

.

How the Spots Rate for Fishing
(5 is the highest)

	Rating	Inlet	Jetty	Fly Fishing	ORV Advisable
1. Okracoke Inlet	🐟🐟	✗	✗		✗
2. Hatteras Inlet	🐟🐟🐟	✗	✗		✗
3. Cape Point at Buxton	🐟🐟🐟🐟	✗			
4 Oregon Inlet	🐟🐟	✗			
5. Pamlico Sound Shallows	🐟	✗	✗	✗	
6. Outer Banks Fishing Piers	🐟				
7. Hatteras Open Beach	🐟				
8. Assateague Island N.S.	🐟🐟🐟				
9. Assateague Barrier Islands	🐟🐟🐟	✗			
10. Ocean City	🐟	✗	✗		
11. Indian River Inlet	🐟🐟🐟	✗	✗		
12. Delaware State Parks	🐟	✗			
13. Lower Delaware River	🐟🐟	✗			
14. Schuylkill River	🐟	✗			
15. Upper Delaware River	🐟🐟	✗			
16. New Jersey Piers	🐟				
17. Cape May Point	🐟🐟🐟	✗	✗		
18. Hereford Inlet	🐟	✗	✗	✗	
19. Townsend's Inlet	🐟🐟	✗	✗	✗	
20. Corson's Inlet	🐟🐟	✗	✗	✗	
21. Great Egg Harbor	🐟	✗	✗	✗	
22. Absecon Inlet Plus	🐟🐟	✗	✗	✗	
23. Graveling Point	🐟🐟	✗	✗	✗	
24. Mystic Islands	🐟🐟	✗		✗	
25. Brigantine Inlet	🐟🐟🐟	✗		✗	

		Rating	Inlet	Jetty	Fly Fishing	ORV Advisable
26.	Beach Haven (Hole Gate)	🐟🐟🐟	✗	✗	✗	✗
27.	Long Beach Island	🐟🐟	✗	✗		
28.	Barnegat Inlet South Jetty	🐟🐟🐟🐟	✗	✗		
29.	Barnegat Inlet North Jetty	🐟🐟🐟🐟	✗	✗		✗
30.	Sedge Island	🐟🐟	✗	✗	✗	
31.	Island Beach	🐟🐟🐟🐟🐟	✗	✗		✗
32.	Point Pleasant Canal	🐟🐟	✗			
33.	Brick Beach	🐟🐟				
34.	Manasquan Inlet	🐟	✗	✗		
35.	Shark River Inlet	🐟🐟🐟	✗	✗		
36.	Manasquan to Long Branch	🐟🐟🐟	✗	✗		
37.	Sandy Hook Point	🐟🐟🐟🐟🐟	✗			✗
38.	Lighthouse Bay	🐟				
39.	Piermont Pier	🐟🐟				
40.	Croton Bay	🐟🐟🐟				
41.	Troy Dam	🐟🐟🐟				
42.	Manhattan	🐟				
43.	Breezy Point	🐟🐟🐟🐟	✗	✗		✗
44.	Silver Point	🐟	✗	✗		
45.	Point Lookout	🐟	✗	✗		
46.	Jones Inlet	🐟🐟	✗	✗		
47.	Captree State Park	🐟	✗		✗	
48.	Fire Island	🐟🐟🐟	✗			✗
49.	Moriches Inlet	🐟🐟🐟	✗	✗	✗	
50.	Shinnecock Inlet	🐟🐟	✗	✗		✗
51.	Nepeague Beach	🐟🐟	✗			✗
52.	Montauk Point	🐟🐟🐟🐟🐟	✗			
53.	Orient Point	🐟🐟	✗			
54.	Long Island North Shore	🐟	✗	✗		
55.	Sunken Meadow	🐟	✗	✗	✗	

		Rating	Inlet	Jetty	Fly Fishing	ORV Advisable
56.	LILCO Northport	🐟	✗	✗		
57.	Calf Pasture Point	🐟🐟	✗	✗	✗	
58.	Cedar Point and Compo Beach	🐟🐟🐟	✗	✗	✗	
59.	Penfield Reef	🐟🐟🐟	✗		✗	
60.	Saint Mary's Beach, Ash Creek	🐟🐟	✗			
61.	Housatonic River	🐟	✗	✗	✗	
62.	Silver Sands State Park	🐟🐟🐟	✗		✗	
63.	Enfield Dam	🐟🐟🐟				
64.	Hammonasset Beach State Park	🐟🐟	✗	✗		
65.	Cornfield Point	🐟🐟🐟	✗		✗	
66.	Conn. DEP Headquarters	🐟🐟	✗	✗	✗	
67.	Sound View Beach	🐟🐟🐟	✗		✗	
68.	Niantic River	🐟🐟🐟	✗	✗	✗	
69.	Harkness Memorial	🐟🐟🐟	✗		✗	
70.	Thames River, Norwich	🐟🐟				
71.	Bluff Point State Park	🐟	✗			

ACKNOWLEDGMENTS

The formulation of this book's concept is mine and as far as I know the original *Striper Hot Spots* was the first locations directory ever done for the striper surf. This original catalog of shore fishing locations was published in 1993 under the extreme disadvantages of more limited techniques of communication than are available today. My publisher provided a $500 phone grant, which was promptly exhausted. I was forced to deal with any number of unknown correspondents; and, information for the many locations was either sorely lacking or fraught with evasive efforts to be obscure. In spite of the barriers that prevented my learning, I was able to amass enough data for what was then 100 hot spots to produce a workable text. Since that original project nearly 20 years ago, the first *Striper Hot Spots* has remained the best working directory on the subject with a plethora of knockoff books by other writers who complimented my efforts through imitation.

Today's version, which is directed to the Middle Atlantic states of the Striper Coast, is infinitely more sophisticated through the use of cheaper communication, a coastwide intimacy with the first effort that helped me to recruit support, and Internet use, which provided me with endless sources of information that could easily be supported. Places that I had not seen were enhanced by "flyovers" on Maps Live. I was able to communicate, measure, see and even refine contacts by way of the information highway that did not even begin to provide the information of today. A consequence of these developments is a much more accurate presentation of a location's striper surf viability.

Common to every hot-spot effort has been the support of real people, said that way with the Internet in mind. South to north, I am indebted to Virginian Stan Creighton for giving me some good pointers on where to begin in the study of striper locations; to D. J. Muller, a New Jersey writer who penned a fine book called *The Surfcaster's Guide to the Striper Coast*, for his input on the Outer Banks of North Carolina; and to Michael Jackson at the Fishin' Hole in Salvo on Hatteras Island for his patient explanation of how the striper fishing works at OBX. I was extremely fortunate enough to touch base with Sue Foster of Oyster Bay Tackle, who runs a pair of tackle shops on the Delmarva Peninsula. Talk about somebody who knows fishing! You know it in your gut when you meet them.

The Delaware River fishery unraveled on the Internet for me but I happened to encounter Sebastian Marino, a striperman who beefed up my understanding of this growing fishery and provided great photo support. New Jersey contacts were easy because there are more surfcasters there than flowers in a garden state. Bob D'Amico, publisher of StriperSurf.com and for whom I have been an administrator of a chat room for ten years, was the easiest pickings of all. Bob Ragati of Toms River and his son, Andrew Ragati, helped by adding locations I had missed the first time around. Ragati's intimacy with Island Beach State Park carried New Jersey's top surf fishing opportunity for me along with aerial views in the photos he provided. Patrick O'Donnell of Kearny, New Jersey, shared six breathtaking photos for inclusion in jetty treatments. Walter Hingley, a longtime supporter and friend, gave me what I needed to capture the fun and frolic of Montauk.

Charlie Taylor provided me with a breathtaking Long Island 63-pound schoolie. Perusing my own film archives, I found plenty of striper-philic film exposed by our son, Dick.

Dr. John Waldman, author and scientist, my go-to guy whenever I run up against a blind alley, enabled me to add important spots on a growing Hudson River fishery.

True to the experience I had in 1993, cooperation sought for a better intimacy with Long Island was again evasive. I did have one bait and tackle shop owner explain to me that disclosure of fishing locations there could hurt his business more than help it. Having Breezy Point and Montauk treated as secrets escapes me. We got by with what was learned the first time around as well as what was enhanced by the Internet.

Connecticut was effortless because I had treated it more expansively in the third edition of the original *Striper Hot Spots* and I enjoy more familiarity with it and regulars there. Again, the Internet, a little more experience, and pure luck made it possible to expand. My wife of 52 years, Joyce, with whom I consult on everything that I write from inception to final draft, remains the shadow partner and first-line editor of everything that I do. Scary that I need her so much.

INTRODUCTION

The purpose of this book is to document the finest surfcasting locations on the Striper Coast, from the Outer Banks of North Carolina to the east end of Connecticut. A directory of prime places to fish from shore, it contains directions, geographic considerations, fishing methods in use, incidental species, and favored angling times. There are, of course, any number of shore-fishing locations outside these parameters, but I have chosen the ones in this book because social and natural considerations render them the most reasonable.

The main criteria for the selection of these hot spots are their productivity and accessibility. I define productivity here as a surfcaster's potential for success as compared with other locations. Success, of course, can be based upon the catching of any number of gamefish, and these can be ranked according to species most often sought, those most important. The guiding considerations in species selection, which should surprise no seasoned saltwater angler, are, in rank order: striped bass, bluefish, weakfish, blackfish, fluke, bonito, and porgy. While this leaves out some species, I think the spirit of my intent has been served. Of course, if stripers were the only game in town, we would be limited to them alone. Indeed, with some exceptions, if it isn't a striper spot, it doesn't count. However, so often a place that appeals to one fish appeals to another, as is the case when adding bluefish and weakfish. Similarly, some locations where the striper is locally important have a unique run of another species and the secondary gamefish is often overlooked; still another is famous for blackfish but overlooked for its fine striper fishing. I have tried to cover all that is known.

Another enigma in the preparation of this work is scope—where to begin and end and what to include. It was already too great an area to encompass the entire range of striper fishing from North Carolina to the Canadian border. Thus, the need to have two sets of hot spots evolved—Mid-Atlantic and New England are treated separately in two different directories. The notion that a Delaware surfcaster would have little use for Maine locations when coupled with size begged attention in the formulation of two separate locations directories. Even then, with population centers at the separation point, where should the break between them occur? The Hudson River was a logical geographic consideration but then, for a New York or New Jersey person, Connecticut could be useful. We solved that by including spots for Connecticut in both editions.

Where to begin the south was a bit of a toss-up. There is some striper activity below the Outer Banks and we came close to stretching our attentions another 100 miles down to Cape Fear. Nevertheless, climate, angling interest, and proximity to Chesapeake Bay made the choice a bit thin.

What this book is not is a treatise on surfcasting. You are expected to have learned that elsewhere, or to be engaged in the lifelong pursuit of this knowledge. You are supposed to know how to deal with slick jetties and sloppy salt-chuck—often green, white, and dirty—blowing over the jetty, which are the only causal agents between you and your maker. Korkers, cleats, belts, flotation, and judgment are outside the bounds of this book. It is assumed that you know that surfcasting can be quite dangerous.

It is not enough to list these many places without extensive supportive information. Techniques and conditions play no small part in the formulation of a hot spot, as well as what is needed to make it all work. The selection of technique becomes a case of choosing between what one thinks is best versus what is being done locally. I tend to go with the latter on the assumption that the anglers who frequent a spot know more than I about what works there. No seasoned regular would argue that most places enjoy sets of favored conditions that often improve or ruin the fishing. For instance, a sou'west wind at one spot during a given stage of tide might enhance one's opportunities; conversely, an east wind might ruin all hope on a particular east-facing beach—though not on all east-facing beaches. To make matters more complicated, there might even be an interrelationship between methods and conditions: for example, if everybody says that pink Nockajimas work best at a given place during a southeast wind, that is the way it gets written up. I won't contaminate local doctrine with my own biases unless local notions are outrageous.

Another consideration for inclusion here is that it has never been our intent to document some little hot spot that accommodates two esoteric hardcores doing a striper number alone in the dark of night. This is not because secrecy is important or that I take anyone's threats seriously, but such disclosures would serve no purpose. As a result, public property predominates in a high percentage of hot spots because of its inherent accessibility. Conversely, some places are more popular than they deserve to be simply because they accommodate greater numbers of fishermen.

The notion of "spot burning" is applied by some anglers to the act of publicizing a fishing location. The logic employed is that the less is known about where fishing is going on, the less competition is likely to ensue over fishing there. What many seem to want is obscure and overlooked fishing hot spots that are devoid of other anglers so that those multitudes may enjoy them themselves. Notwithstanding, such utopias are not really attainable in a densely populated geographic setting as can be found in what is now known as our Striper Coast. Indeed, the true secrets of the shorelines frequented by knowing disciples of the striper surf are not where to fish but rather, how to fish them. As long as we deal with mapped shorelines with bird's-eye views, global positioning, mass media, Internet communication and a plethora of printed media devoted to striper fishing, I fail to see any true secrets, especially when so many of the well-documented locations are public property promulgated for recreation. All that is being done here is your legwork.

In addition to the obvious interest in striper surf locations illustrated in the success of this book—printed eleven times in its original form—I once met a surfman who sought to determine if his spot was covered by checking in his local, Long Island library. When he looked it up he found the page had been torn out.

The late Frank Woolner, who was my first editor and mentor 40 years ago, wrote a sensitive and telling piece about this very subject back when Sophia Loren was first learning about men. In his article "To Kill a Lake" Woolner lamented the agonies of publicizing a great and somewhat private fishing spot. His point was that those of us who write about exciting opportunities in the field are apt to draw the multitudes and destroy the very thing we love most. Still, you can only do so much of the gimmickry of old-time war correspondents "somewhere in Southeast Asia" or the angling scribe's "a small stream in Allegheny County."

Thus, discussions that pinpoint what is good become matters of conscience for outdoor writers struggling with objectivity, secrecy and what others are likely to say about it. Location, as the real estate agents like to say, is everything. Also, the old saw about information really being the farmer's daughter hits you right between the eyes: If you don't do it someone else will.

Striper Hot Spots is nothing more than some badly needed musical chairs that engages the same number of seats while changing the rumps. In most cases intimacies of a hot spot spring from the contact tip that can be cogent. Even so, no reporter with a modicum of objectivity would fail to see the red alert of his BS-Meter when a bait and tackle dealer says that the fishing is "99 percent bait," and when asked where an angler might get that bait, the answer is "here." This broadening of people's available locations will have no adverse influence upon the quality of the sport.

Each hot spot has a contact that is intimate with the spot above it. In most cases much of the information on that spot came from that bait and tackle shop. Be mindful that with the passage of time some of these shops may go out, their phone numbers might change, or they might not be open when you call. A wise choice would be to call the next contact listed. Keep in mind that while digesting what is said about the fishing, angling areas, like ski areas, always have more packed powder than is really there.

Nearly all to whom I spoke were truthful, said so when they didn't know, and told me where I could find out. They were usually thrilled to participate in this endeavor, which should certainly outlast me and probably some of them. Smart enough to know, without being reminded, that they were contributing something, they were enthusiastic, truthful, and flattered to have the opportunity.

Examining some of the common qualities of these 71 locations yielded some not-so-surprising statistics. For instance, 62 percent of them are inlets. I have long said, always practiced, and on many occasions written on the beauty of inlets as places where bait lured great gamefish. Because so many inlets are flanked by jetties to preserve their integrity, a high percent of the spots ended up being flanked by jetties. That 38 percent of the spots host fly fishing speaks more of the trendy nature of the activity. The truth is that one could fly fish them all, but I tried to stay with either personal experience or respondents' knowledge. The use of over-sand vehicles is permitted in 15 percent of the places, but that is not to say that a "beach buggy" is needed to fish there in all cases.

A dozen other spots have been rewritten extensively with more pertinent information. In response to the overwhelming interest in fly fishing, we have made a greater effort to identify the growing list of suitable fly-fishing locations. Fly fishers should watch for the special fly icon, which designates hot spots known for fly fishing. Again each of the hot spots has a contact tip—a fishing shop you can call in the proximity that should know more than any of us about the conditions there.

The hot spots are listed in geographical order, from south to north, as the migrating species travel in spring. So if you don't like to read a book in order, or if you just plain like to jump around, feel free to do that here.

When I take into account all the factors—size, accessibility, species availability, water movement and depth, facing directions, and overall production in terms of fish caught—each hot spot begs for some sort of value judgment that defines it more objectively. Indeed, to keep the information that gathers on a particular spot in control, a rating system serves as a means of boiling it all down. Here, I must quickly create a clear separation between a 5-mile hot spot at the mouth of a river, like the Delaware, and some obscure beach a mile long that is rarely fished—and all the levels in between. What springs from those thoughts is that Montauk Point is rated a five while a relatively unknown pier is a one. Of course, such judgments can become mighty subjective while inspiring heated disagreements—as often based on local pride as on protectionist sentiments. With those thoughts in mind, I must apologize in advance for decisions that might seem skewed to some knowing regular out there. My rating system, which I want you to take with a grain of salt, breaks down as follows:

Rating	Number of Hot Spots with That Rating
5	3
4	4
3	21
2	23
1	20

STRIPER HOT SPOTS

MIDDLE ATLANTIC

NORTH CAROLINA

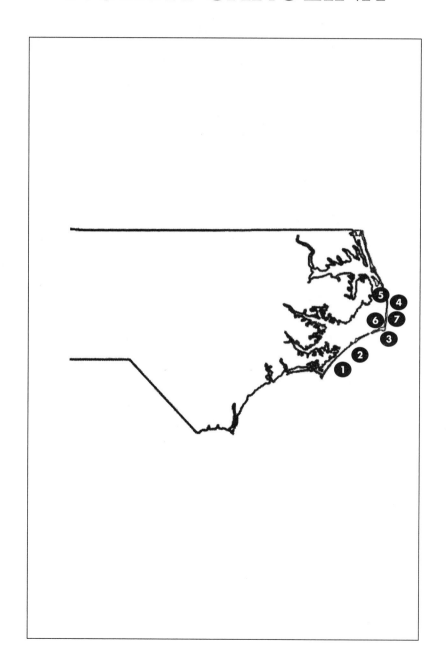

North Carolina
Cape Hatteras/Outer Banks
of North Carolina

This Cape Hatteras run of public shore is probably the strongest southern surfcasting location on the Striper Coast. Certainly, it vies with Cape Cod when compared with anything this side of the Canadian border. While there are miles of fishable beach between them, the most prominent hot spots, what I call the Hatteras Five, have been grouped here south to north. Everything said here can be said about all of them.

The Hatteras National Seashore starts below Nags Head and runs for 72 miles south. The entire distance is managed variably with closures that respond to bird nesting, beach erosion, and social considerations meant to accommodate seasonal beach use. Consequently, some sections are always closed to ORV use; others are open to beach driving or Soundside trails year-round; others enjoy seasonal access from September 15 to May 15 when fishing is best. The full seashore is marked off with ramp numbers, which approximate their distance in miles down Route NC-12 until the end at Ramp #72. There are three Ranger Station/Visitor Centers: Bodie Island, Hatteras, and Ocracoke Island. These are also the locations of the region's three lighthouses. NPS also offers three campgrounds at approximate miles 4, 48, and 68. Three fishing piers that reach out into the Atlantic are placed at Mile Post numbers 6, 12, and 18½. All uses and regulatory issues are well marked by NPS.

Beach buggies are advisable in order to experience the full thrust of Outer Banks surfcasting opportunity. The National Park Service has not required ORV permits, but that could soon happen if permits become a part of a pending lawsuit requiring an Off Road Vehicle Plan for OBX. It should all be settled by the time you read this. Much of the shore can be accessed with a family auto on adjacent highways but the better fishing spots, the inlets and Cape Point, are impossible to walk.

This area is where an annual staging of the lion's share of striped bass takes place during winter. It has become famous for its seasonal boat fishing off of Corolla and on south to Cape Lookout by the local charter fleet and where the largest number of the biggest bass are taken every winter. The All-Tackle World Record bluefish, taken by James Hussey in 1972 weighing 31 pounds, 12 ounces, was taken off of Cape Hatteras. Fishing from boats here is outrageously good in the face of being controversial when the numbers of large breeders removed each season are taken into account. For the surfcaster the fishing does not compare to that which takes place offshore. However, there is a viable enough striper fishery that does find itself within beach range just often enough for treatment here.

What is enigmatic about the entire area and its attendant striper fishing opportunities is that many seasons the main body of returning migrating stripers do not come this far south if waters to the north stay warm. The striper run is highly dependent upon seasonal temperatures and early cold weather is needed to drive both bait and bass further south. Otherwise they stop at Virginia Beach or thereabouts 100 miles north of there.

Red drum have done as much for Outer Banks' reputation as a surf fishing destination as have stripers. As a consequence, methods utilized in drum fishing are reflected somewhat in the methods that are applied to stripers. However, seasons of opportunity are different for the two species with only a slight overlap, particularly in fall, and some years no overlap at all.

Angling methods for Cape Hatteras utilize more bait fishing on the bottom than artificials. Anglers do a lot of chunking. High surf—the wind always blows—heavy sinkers, and the anticipation of larger fish, be they drum or striper, causes knowing regulars to fish much heavier with longer surf rods than at many other striper hot spots. When fishing is good, bait is sometimes sold out for the many surfcasters who responded to the call of a blitz.

Well-known New Jersey surfcasting writer DJ Muller has been going there with his family to fish since he was a kid. In his fine book, *The Surfcaster's Guide to the Striper Coast,* he writes that "The Outer Banks of North Carolina is more a state of mind than just a fishing location." I asked DJ to tell us more: "One of the most beautiful terrains, of the many along the striper coast, are the sandy shores of the Outer Banks of North Carolina. It is a location where large bodies of striped bass winter giving the shore fishing there potential to be off the charts. Known for its legendary red drum runs, the area from Oregon Inlet south to Ocracoke gives the surfcaster looking for large striped bass a fair chance at some late-season action."

When striper fishing in Hatteras, the name of the game is "big" and bait. Big equipment is used for big bass. Most bass caught in Hatteras will be over 20 pounds and the majority will be caught on bait, usually fresh menhaden or bunker.

The standard equipment for OBX is conventional reels accompanied by a 12-foot-long conventional rod. Long casts into the rips are needed for success and the long rod helps you in that department. Also, the big stick helps with leveraging a big bass as well as navigating it along the beach.

The hard rule of line in Hatteras is monofilament. Braid is frowned upon there because oftentimes lines cross and braid is not a tangle-friendly line. Twenty-pound-test mono fits the bill perfectly. The rig used is usually a 13/0 or 14/0 Mustad circle hook with a very short lead of 100-pound-test mono to a barrel swivel. Most of the shops sell the rigs at affordable prices. The running line holds a fishfinder rig, and a sinker from 6 to 8 ounces is a good starting point. The bait is cut into small chunks. The short rig and small bait size is necessary for casting distance. The small bait and short leader make for less tumble of the sinker and bait on the cast thus giving added distance.

The places you want to target in Hatteras are, in general terms, Oregon Inlet's north shoreline—a place accessible by 4x4; the Point in Buxton, where the famed Cape Hatteras lighthouse stands over your left shoulder watching you; and Hatteras Inlet at the end of Hatteras Island. It is important to know that there are no guarantees in Hatteras as the fishing can be hit or miss but you will never catch a cow if you don't roll up your sleeves and try.

When using the various bait and tackle shop contacts listed for each respective hot spot, check around and gain a consensus because they all have a good feel for what is going on.

In the shrinking world of the striper surf, the traditions of mid-watch hunts, comradery, beach-buggies and salt spray enjoyed here are consistent with what those who are reading this have come to love. Places like these are what you should be looking for.

A fishing license is not needed on the charter boats or fishing piers because both have blanket licenses that cover visiting anglers, but for fishing the beach a North Carolina saltwater license is required.

1

Okracoke Inlet
Cape Hatteras National Seashore
Okracoke, North Carolina

BEST MONTHS TO FISH: November, December, and April.

RECOMMENDED METHODS: Cut baits comprised of either menhaden or mullet are the standard. Some live eels are used early in the fall season and there is some tin casting during daylight hours.

FISH YOU CAN EXPECT TO CATCH: Stripers, and bluefish during autumn; red drum in spring.

HOW TO GET THERE: South on Route 12 to land's end. Because Okracoke is on an island, if you come from the south it is necessary to take the ferry out of Swanquarter, which can be reached via Route 264 on the mainland. There is also another ferry out of Atlantic on Route 12 south of there. Use of a beach-buggy is advisable.

Because this spot is the southernmost of this book's range, many years it does not have as good a run of bass as can be found to the north. Often water temperatures stay warm enough to the north and with good bait above, the bass fail to show in this area. The fall run simply stops north of there if fish move into Chesapeake Bay.

There is plenty of moving water here because the inlet serves Pamlico Sound. Consequently, the spot is not as tide dependent as some inlets. As long as you are fishing after dark, you have a good shot at having your chunk picked up on the sandy bottom by a decent striper. Big fish feed more aggressively at night. Fresh usable bait is often a problem in this region so it is advisable to bring whatever you have in your freezer that could suffice on the outside chance the shops are out.

Other months, April and October being the best, red drum as large as 60 inches are the local targets of opportunity. Methods for drum are the same as those for stripers. The All-Tackle World Record Spanish mackerel, weighing 13 pounds, was caught here.

CONTACT TIP: O'Neal's Dockside Tackle Shop, Ocracoke, (252) 928-1111.

2
Hatteras Inlet
Cape Hatteras National Seashore
Hatteras, North Carolina

BEST MONTHS TO FISH: November, December, and April some years.
RECOMMENDED METHODS: Cut baits comprised of either menhaden or mullet are the standard. Some live eels are used early in the fall season and there is some tin during daylight hours.

"OBX" is the wintering ground of big Atlantic stripers.

FISH YOU CAN EXPECT TO CATCH: Stripers, and bluefish during autumn; red drum in spring.

HOW TO GET THERE: Straight down Route 12, follow your nose.

Influences on the fishing, methods and even results are largely the same as with Ocracoke except that this spot has a slight edge in that it is more accessible, in spite of the need for use of a beach-buggy. The same people using the same methods frequent all four of these adjacent spots, which are under 70 miles apart.

No doubt there is a lot of communication between those plying the waters of them all. Conditional to Hatteras Inlet is that the prevailing summer wind, which is the southwest, adversely affects the fishing in most cases. Still, of the three inlets, excluding Cape Point at Buxton, which needs special treatment, Hatteras is the most popular. The All-Tackle World Record red drum weighing 94 pounds was caught here.

CONTACT TIP: Frisco Rod and Gun, Hatteras, (252) 995-5366.

3

Cape Point at Buxton
Cape Hatteras National Seashore
Buxton, North Carolina

BEST MONTHS TO FISH: November, December and April, May.

RECOMMENDED METHODS: Cut baits comprised of either menhaden or mullet are the standard. There is some tin casting during daylight hours and live eel fishing at night.

FISH YOU CAN EXPECT TO CATCH: Stripers, and bluefish during autumn; red drum in spring.

HOW TO GET THERE: Take the ORV road off Route 12 and keep the lighthouse on your left going on.

While this is the only non-inlet of the Hatteras locations, it ranks as the highest in surfcasting potential. The reason for this is the "point" of Cape Hatteras Point is formed and maintained by the

Surfmen view Cape Point as the best of the Outer Banks.

collision of two of the largest ocean currents in the Atlantic—the Gulf Stream from the south (South Atlantic Bight) and the Labrador Current from the north (Mid-Atlantic Bight). With the addition of a little weather, the clapping of the two masses of moving water creates quite a nature spectacle, the waves of each flow getting pushy kicking froth skyward in the creation of a sandbar that reaches seaward continuing below the surface for miles. Those exciting photos of Cape Hatteras we've all seen were likely taken here. The violence of this meeting of the seas is best illustrated by its known moniker, "The Graveyard of the Atlantic." If you doubt it, note the partially submerged hulks in the surf and the decaying shipwrecks scattered along the shore well up into the dunes. It is a nasty place for shipwrecks but a dandy for surfcasting. A serious issue in the development of the fishing is the huge temperature gradient that springs from the two currents. One can observe a difference of as much as ten or fifteen degrees in the seawater temperature at Cape Point. Hence, one can envision shaking hands on the bar with the variety of northern and southernmost species of gamefish. One time or another there is everything here—pompano, tarpon, two species of drum, bluefish, Spanish mackerel, cobia, croaker, weakfish, speckled trout and of course the wily striper, better known as rockfish in these parts. Anglers catch critters they can't even identify. Still, it is the white water clapping skyward that marks itself indelibly in your memory.

Surfcasters rely upon chunk baits (what your uncle called cut bait back when only boys had tattoos) sinkered to the bottom but allowed to swing and drag in the current during night hours. When birds are working during daylight in blitzy conditions there is some tin fishing for dealing with wind and distance. Unlike the rest of the Striper Coast, there is little plug fishing in use here. And, they will kill you if you try to fly fish, then use your body parts for chunking.

The best set of conditions is when the tide is dropping and the wind is blowing hard, which is all the time. We would have rated this spot a top-notch five, but some years the stripers don't come this far south. At this end of the Striper Coast water temperatures are a big determinant for the quality of striper runs.

CONTACT TIP: The Fishin Hole in Salvo, (252) 987-2351.

4
Oregon Inlet
Cape Hatteras National Seashore
Wanchese, North Carolina

BEST MONTHS TO FISH: November, December and April.

RECOMMENDED METHODS: Cut baits comprised of either menhaden or mullet are the standard. Some live eels are used early in the fall season and there is some tin during daylight hours.

FISH YOU CAN EXPECT TO CATCH: Stripers, and bluefish during autumn; red drum in spring.

HOW TO GET THERE: Take the ORV road once in sight of the bridge to your south.

Fishing here is very much like Hatteras and Ocracoke Inlet both in timing and methods. However, they are far enough apart to sometimes provide significantly different fishing. Consequently, OBX regulars are watching them all. Likely a more northerly placement could be an advantage some years if stripers are reluctant to move south. It is also the first of the three inlets and much closer for those driving south on Route 12 at M.P. (Mile Post) 4.

CONTACT TIP: Red Drum Tackle in Buxton, N.C., (252) 995-5414.

5

Pamlico Sound Shallows
Cape Hatteras National Seashore
Nags Head, North Carolina

BEST MONTHS TO FISH: March through January; summer is best.

RECOMMENDED METHODS: Fly fishing or light tackle spinning.

FISH YOU CAN EXPECT TO CATCH: School stripers, blues, speckled trout, gray weakfish, croakers and kingfish.

HOW TO GET THERE: Variable locations along Route 12 where it is possible to pull off.

This is a collection of spots on the inland or Pamlico Sound side of the Route 12/Hatteras Barrier Beach that are spaced for 50 miles south from Bodie Island Light to Hatteras Inlet. We lump these together because of the similarities in both their access and fishing methods. It is a borderline issue as to whether they should have been treated separately, but they are similar enough to be treated as one.

Pamlico shallows hold great light tackle for small fish opportunities.

I counted no less than six commonly waded locations: Bodie Island Light, Herring Shoals Slough, Propeller Slough, Green Island Slough, Dredge Slough, and Shot Tower. A shore fisher who checks all six of these out in the deep night is bound to find action somewhere along the stretch of protected backwater edges of the sound among the many sloughs that can be found there. All are accessible by Route 12 or the ORV Soundside Trail or combinations of the two roads. The channel of the first is behind Bodie Island Light (4 miles); Herring Shoal Island is another three miles south; Propeller Shoal is at the south end of the Oregon Inlet Fishing Center; Green Island is on the south side of the Oregon Inlet bridge. Dredge Slough is roughly six miles down just short of Avon; and, Shot Tower is just south of the Hatteras Inlet Coast Guard Station. Strong currents and sudden drop-offs make all these spots dangerous for anglers who don't know the ropes.

Unlike the front beach where surf and ocean currents set the pace in angling for the use of much heavier gear, the back side of the Hatteras barrier beach is perfect for the use of lighter tackle for smaller fish. It is also an alternative to the front in the event of big and bad water that can present itself at times in ocean fishing. A deep channel runs within wading distance of the shore for much of the stretch. Tides are slight enough all through here that currents are on the mild side but strong enough to lure gamefish.

The variety of species that can be taken here is astounding. You spend more time trying to guess what you hooked than catching them. Regulars find the fly fishing productive with floating or intermediate lines most nights. Nevertheless, I would advise a backup fly line with a high sink rate for dealing with some of the heavy currents if you want to find the bottom. Any of the streamer patterns in use elsewhere should suffice. Lean in the direction of the old standards—Deceiver variations with a few shrimp and crab patterns for dealing with pickiness. Spin fishermen can use smaller swimmers or bucktails for dealing with heavier currents where you find them. Small poppers, as is the case everywhere else, work during the day. Fishing is good either tide but I think the drop in tide has an edge.

Sunrise boat traffic—which puts the fish down—is so robust that I would not advise early-morning fishing, relying more upon the deep night for the tranquility and sound of slurping gamefish swilling on the small stuff common to estuaries. We ranked this low, not because of the fishing, but rather because of the panfish nature of the opportunity when compared to the monsters out front. Up north we call these "schoolie spots."

CONTACT TIP: Red Drum Tackle Shop, Buxton, (252) 995-5414.

6

Outer Banks Fishing Piers
Along Route 12 from Frisco North
Outer Banks, North Carolina

BEST MONTHS TO FISH: Stripers—November and April. Other stuff year long except for winter.

RECOMMENDED METHODS: Bottom baits from local pier tackle shops.

FISH YOU CAN EXPECT TO CATCH: Stripers in season; blues, speckled trout, cobia, pompano and king mackerel, among others.

HOW TO GET THERE: All locations are spread along state Route 12 with various points of access.

Informally known as the world capital of pier fishing, as recently as 1996 there were 32 fishing piers in this region. By 2001, thanks to hurricanes, there were 25. Today 19 remain fishable. The following only address the most popular. Six fishing piers are spread along this highway that reach various distances out into the Atlantic, usually around 700 feet. Pier end depths, tide depending, vary from 12 to 15 feet. Most offer full fishing services complete with pier access and tackle shops, some with restaurants and cottage rentals. Nags Head Fishing Pier has a motto, "You hook em— we cook em!" They are not kidding as they will cook your catch at the Pier House Restaurant. There are stripers in season and the variety of local gamefish available is astounding. Most have tackle rentals and are capable of filling your every need—bottom rigs, rods and reels, top-water lures, even advice. This is not kid fishing as they commonly catch cobia and king mackerel up to 60 pounds, bigger in some cases. They offer fishing around the clock including nights. This is no-hassle pay-as-you-fish for pier use.

The fishing piers start opening in March on weekends, accommodating later hours and more days as the fishing improves. By the late May Memorial Day holiday, it is all in full tilt bailing of gamefish. They start closing down around the end of November, depending upon the fishing.

The privately operated piers all have fee schedules that vary somewhat but to give you a feel of prices they usually offer a $10 day pass and roughly $25 for three days, $60 for a week, a season pass for around the low $200 give or take. Kids under 12 half price.

You can also bridge fish from the catwalk on the south side of Oregon Inlet or from a small bridge at Manteo Causeway at Nags Head. Nearby there is a public fishing pier. Just turn down the road at Pirate's Cove Marina and swing back under the bridge.

Here is a list, south to north, with contact numbers, of the piers that are bound to keep you awake at night:

Cape Hatteras Fishing Pier, Frisco, 6:00 A.M. to 11 P.M., (252) 986-2533.

Avon Fishing Pier, Avon, 6:00 A.M. to 12:00 A.M., (252) 995-5480.

Hatteras Island Fishing Pier, Rodanthe, 6:30 A.M. to 12:00 A.M., (252) 987-2323.

Outer Banks Fishing Pier, MP 18½, South Nags Head, open 24 hours, (252) 441-5740.

Nags Head Fishing Pier, MP 12, Nags Head, open 24 hours, (252) 441-5141.

Avalon Fishing Pier, MP 6, Kill Devil Hills, 5:00 A.M. to 2:00 A.M., (252) 441-7494.

7

Hatteras Open Beach
Rodanthe to Salvo
Cape Hatteras National Seashore
North Carolina

BEST MONTHS TO FISH: November and April.

RECOMMENDED METHODS: Stout bait rods with chunk bottom baits.

Migrating gamefish have to pass the open beaches.

FISH YOU CAN EXPECT TO CATCH: Stripers, blues, some red drum, some speckled trout.

HOW TO GET THERE: Any pull-off on Route 12 in the vicinity of M.P. 23 to M.P. 34.

The outer beach between Rodanthe and Salvo has variable sloughs and gullies within casting range along the beach that occasionally appeal to whatever species are passing the Outer Banks. An attractive aspect of this angling choice is that you fish where you can park and access the shore where it is likely that you can fish away from the crowds.

Probably the most decisive issue in your fishing is the timing involved. When migrations are on whatever is going past is bound to be in lurking in the often exciting structure that can form here. Storm-driven winds, tides, and seasonal activity all play a part in the run. Consequently, much of the bottom structure is highly changeable where one season it is exciting enough to give a beach reader a bible full of study and the next year it is flat as a pancake. Selection of the right place to drop your bait and sinker is no small part of the game. The only thing that can be said about any bad fishing is that summers are slow in this region. In addition, don't even think about striped bass. It is a case of the right season, the freshest bait, and the most well-placed cast. If you can't handle what you have hooked, it is probably a red drum. Hang on!

CONTACT TIP: Hatteras Jack Bait and Tackle, Rodanthe, (252) 987-2428.

Here is a list of all the known bait and tackle shops you can call that serve the Outer Banks:

Ocracoke Island
O'Neal's Dockside Tackle Shop, (252) 928-1111
Tradewinds Tackle Shop, (252) 928-5491
Hatteras Island
Hatteras Jack Bait and Tackle, (252) 987-2428
The Fishin' Hole, (252) 987-2351
Frank and Fran's, (252) 995-4171
Dillon's Corner, (252) 995-5083
Red Drum Tackle Shop, (252) 995-5414
Frisco Rod and Gun, (252) 995-5366
Frisco Tackle, (252) 995-4361
The Roost, (252) 986-2213

Northern Beaches

Corolla Bait and Tackle, (252) 453-9500
TW's Bait and Tackle, (252) 453-3339
Fishin Fever Bait and Tackle, (252) 480-3474
TI's Bait and Tackle, (252) 441-3166
TW's Bait and Tackle, (252) 441-4807
Fishing Unlimited, (252) 441-5028
Whalebone Tackle, (252) 441-7413

DELMARVA

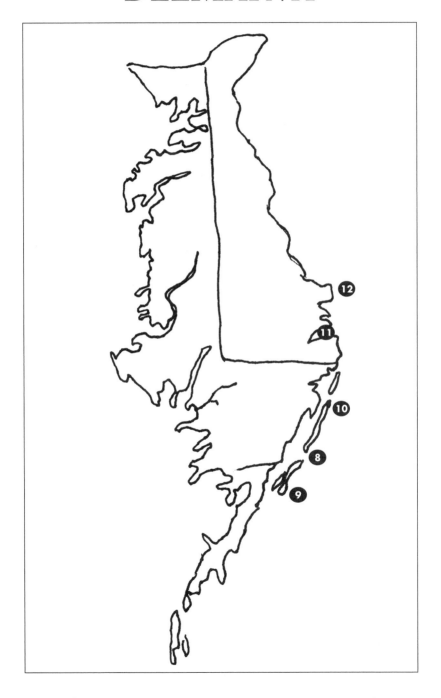

The Delmarva Peninsula

Outsiders commonly fail to understand the source of the regional name Delmarva. This idea came to me while talking about the Eastern Shore with a Hatteras contact. That person was astonished to learn that the region's name was a clip of Delaware, Maryland, and Virginia. Thus this Eastern Shore region is bounded by three states that traverse over 120 miles of oceanside shore from Cape Charles to Cape Henlopen. Comprised of 5 spots treated in this examination, there are enough locations missed here to keep you fishing for a lifetime. No one could ever fish it all, and even the cursory examination that we have done is a monumental task.

Fortunately, I was able to call upon Sue Foster, who runs a pair of tackle ships—Oyster Bay Tackle in Ocean City and Fenwick Tackle on Fenwick Island—for the intimacy with the region needed to treat it as accurately as possible. It takes a townie who knows the ropes about how and where to do the job right, and she does. That said, the hundreds of creeks, marshes, tidal rivers and narrows-inspired currents between the many islands are enough on their own for another book.

There is an interesting southern component in place here that I find strange and begs examination by a Yankee observer like myself who fishes only one season up north. There are two seasons enjoyed here where the glamour species like stripers, bluefish, and drum are fished during the colder months and the small stuff of summer—flounder, spot and weakfish—are sought during the warmer ones. With so many species in evidence in the region, it is a challenge to confine the scope of this work to striped bass or as they say, "rockfish."

Even once we zero in on the rockfish, the issues are not any more simple nearer to the Chesapeake than the waters of my native New England. The average air temperature has a profound influence upon the water temperature that is the determinant of whether they have a good run of stripers any given year. If the water is warm in summer, which is what they expect, the bass migrate north; but if, on the other hand, it is a cool summer they keep more of their fish as cool water appeals to them. This, in fact, happened one recent cool year when they had big bass all season. Similarly, how good their fishing is in fall or spring is a function of water temperature. Keep in mind that in the wintering grounds off the coast of Hatteras, which are often outside the three-mile economic zone, there is less fishing for the brutes that stripermen all lust over. So it is for Delmarva striper-philes—about water temperature.

On first examination a certain envy over their angling opportunity sets in, but closer scrutiny of their best months for striper fishing shows that they actually have less time than those, say, who are fishing Cape Cod. Still, it ends up being about the same at five months. Only near the Chesapeake is their season split.

The southern end of the Striper Coast shows a greater propensity for bait fishing than that in evidence up north. As in the north, there is some bait fishing, so there are some artificials in use in the south. Yet, leanings clearly indicate a difference. There is even, or so it seems, a transitional part of the Striper Coast where a shifting from bottom baits to lures is evident.

All the southern states exempt pier and charter boat anglers from needing a fishing license, but a saltwater license is needed on the beaches for each state.

Here is a list of the Ocean City Bait and Tackle shops that are bound to know what's running in the region:

AKE Marine, (410) 213-0421
Delmarva Sports Center, (410) 213-2840
Elliot's Hardware, (410) 289-6123
Harbor Tackle, (410) 213-9365
Oyster Bay Tackle Shop, (410) 524-3433
Shantytown Fishing Pier, (410) 213-1926
Skip's Bait and Tackle Shop, (410) 289-8555
Sunset Provisions LLC, (410) 213-0081

8

Assateague Island National Seashore
Ocean City, Maryland, and Virginia Eastern Shore

BEST MONTHS TO FISH: Stripers—October, November, December, April and May. Other stuff year long.

RECOMMENDED METHODS: Bottom baits with some artificial lures.

FISH YOU CAN EXPECT TO CATCH: Stripers, blues, weakfish, flounder, kingfish, black drum and red drum.

HOW TO GET THERE: From the north take U.S. 50 east across the Bay Bridge, then south to Salisbury, Maryland, where you'll pick up U.S. 13 south and then Route 175 east to Chincoteague Island. When you get to the island, turn left at the light onto Main Street, then right on Maddox Boulevard. From the south after the Bay Bridge Tunnel head north on U.S. 13

then turn right on Route 175 east. Once on the island turn left at the light onto Main Street then right onto Maddox Boulevard. It's easy.

Stretching south from Ocean City, Maryland, Assateague Island National Seashore is 37 miles of barrier island managed both in Maryland and Virginia. Roughly 20 miles of beach is mainland accessible. The other 17 miles are islands, which are accessible only by boat. (See the next spot, #9, Assateague Barrier Islands.) The north end of the seashore is a more reasonable destination where there are ORV-accessible sections in season.

You may get lucky and catch something in late April but the month of May (around Mother's Day) is usually when better action is seen down here. Rockfish, local parlance for striped bass, are the big deal. Unless it is an unusually warm and early spring, many don't even try to fish the surf until May but stripers are leaving Chesapeake Bay for their migration north and things really pick up fast as the seasons change. Parking lots one and four get a lot of play. The summer fishing for other species ain't none too shabby either. In recent years waters in the region have been kingfish heaven. Gray weakfish, which are highly cyclical anyway, can be off but that is another story.

Popular baits used in bottom fishing include peeler and mole crabs, shrimp, clams, mullet and bunker chunks. As you come north, and it seems to start here, you always want to have a good supply of lures for casting in the event you run into breaking fish on the top. Play it safe.

Assateague Island has both its Maryland and Virginia ORV areas open year-round for off-road beach recreation. The Maryland portion has an ORV zone 12 miles in length, with a

145-vehicle limit. Each end of the island limits the maximum number of vehicles that can be on the beach at any one time. The Virginia portion of the ORV area has several miles open year-round but does close its extreme southern region known as "the hook" from March 15th–September 1st for the nesting piping plover, which is an endangered species. The vehicle limit on the remaining 1.5-mile beach drops to 18 at that time of the year. If any endangered piping plovers decide to nest on that portion of the off-road beach, there are bypass routes that are set up to avoid the birds, but the area still remains open for the season. The 145-vehicle limit is reached early on the weekends and often goes to a one-off/one-on system.

The off-road permit is good for both the Virginia and Maryland ends of Assateague Island and there is a $70 annual permit fee. There are no weekly or other short-term permits. Off-road vehicles must be "street legal" (motorcycles and ATVs are not allowed). You will need to present your registration card. You need a low-pressure tire gauge (it's recommended to let the air out to 15 pounds or so for the soft sand). There are air pumps near the off-road entrance. A shovel, jack, a board to support the jack in the sand (12" square minimum, ¾" plywood or 1½" hardwood), and a tow rope or chain (substantial capacity, 10' minimum length) are also required. Fines are charged for each piece of missing required equipment. The permit is available through the mail (request 3 weeks at least in advance). It can be obtained in person at the Visitor Centers also, (410) 641-3030. While you're shelling out all that cash, Virginia requires a saltwater fishing license.

You can camp on Maryland's side of Assateague Island in the state or national parks. Each has campgrounds that are open in April. The national has cold showers and chemical toilets. The state has more normal bathhouses with hot water and flush toilets. One can camp at the base of the dune and walk over (at a crossover) and be right on the water. I have known folks who have camped there and been 100 to 120 yards (as the crow flies) from tent to surf. They have cautioned that the winds are not to be taken lightly! Any wind over 15 knots from the N or NW will blow your tent down or keep you from getting one up. (Very little wind break on this barrier island.)

Surf fishermen may fish all night on the beach in Maryland, which is accessible 24 hours. In Virginia, fishermen must get an overnight fishing permit at the Visitor Center, since the entrance at the Chincoteague National Wildlife Refuge is closed from 10 P.M. to 5 A.M. during the summer. You must be actively fishing for you and your vehicle to stay on the beach overnight. On the Maryland end, you can return to the campground area if you wish to sleep. To reserve a campsite in the Assateague National Seashore from May 15 through October 15, call (800) 365-2267. Beach permits for a 4-wheel drive: Assateague Island National Seashore, (410) 641-3030.

Don't miss seeing some of the 300 local wild ponies who wander the beaches, pine barrens, and salt marshes. You won't see that anywhere else.

CONTACT TIP: Delmarva Sports Center, Ocean City, (410) 213-2840.

The wild ponies of Assateague are unique to this area.

9
Assateague Barrier Islands
Chincoteague Island
Virginia Eastern Shore

BEST MONTHS TO FISH: Stripers—October, November, December, April and May. Other stuff year long except for winter.

RECOMMENDED METHODS: Bottom baits with some artificial lures. Same as the rest of Assateague.

FISH YOU CAN EXPECT TO CATCH: Stripers, blues, weakfish, flounder, black drum and red drum.

HOW TO GET THERE: Any east turnoffs from Route 113 between Snow Hill and Ocean City will lead to state-operated boat-launching ramps.

The barrier islands are an extension of the Assateague Island National Seashore with largely the same issues in method, opportunity, and available species. However, the difference is that it is a much more private setting in a really inaccessible group of islands to the south that are so difficult to reach that you will see many more fish than people. The only way to get to these 17 islands is to cross from the back by boat. The state maintains numerous boat-launching ramps for that use. Nonetheless, with no bridges out to the islands, most people are not going to bring a boat for use as a taxi to barrier islands. We reduced the rating by one fish for that reason, otherwise fishing would be the same. The surfcasting here is phenomenal, probably because of the remote, reduced activity. It is as pristine today as it was when John Smith arrived. Some of the barrier islands where angling is allowed are Assawoman, Metompkin, Cedar, Cobb, Hog, Smith, Myrtle, Rogue and Mink. Red drum—if you close your eyes they feel like stripers—run famously in June and September.

From Wachapreague to the Bay Bridge Tunnel, anglers who trailer their boats and want to fish the seaside bays and inlets or access the islands have the boat ramps at Wachapreague, Chincoteague, Gargatha Landing, Quinby, Willis Wharf Harbor, Folly Creek, Metomkin, Cape Charles, and Oyster.

What little angling pressure does take place is often directed to the inlets between the islands where there are increases in current flow. I'm told that southeast and east winds enhance the fishing. Things don't really get going until the water temperature is above 50 degrees Farenheit in late March.

DISTRICT VISITOR INFO: Virginia—(757) 336-6577. Maryland—(410) 641-1441.

CONTACT TIP: Skip's Bait and Tackle, Ocean City, (410) 289-8555.

10
Ocean City Potpourri
Ocean City, Maryland

BEST MONTHS TO FISH: Stripers—November, December, April and May. Other stuff year long except for winter.

RECOMMENDED METHODS: Bottom baits such as mullet, squid, live eels, with some artificial lures.

FISH YOU CAN EXPECT TO CATCH: Stripers (rockfish), blues, weakfish, flounder, tautog, trout,sea bass, croaker, and spot.

HOW TO GET THERE: Ocean City is at the end of Route 1 on Maryland's Eastern Shore.

This is a regional collection of hot spots with remarkably similar characteristics that are all in the immediate vicinity of Ocean City. For the intimacies of these commonly fished locations, we talked to Sue Foster, who is high command of Oyster Bay Tackle in Ocean City. Here is a rundown of what she could give us on the fishing.

"Ocean City Inlet has a reliable run of stripers in spring and fall that take eels and lures. The rest of the year it is largely bottom baits like sand fleas, green crabs and clam. Like the nearby Ocean Pier, it is better for the smaller panfish like spot, whiting, and sand perch.

"Oceanic Pier, which is a pay pier at the south end of Philadelphia Avenue, is also near the inlet and has about the same opportunities as the Ocean Pier. They also do a lot of crabbing here starting late summer and into the fall.

"The Route 50 Bridge is famous for its summer flounder fishing during the day with all the other pan species known in the region. However, nights in spring and fall the striper fishing really springs to life because of the lights on the bridge and their resultant shadows. Bridge sharpies scan the shadow edge on the uptide side for black-on-gray striper silhouettes that are facing the tide to ambush forage species. This is a highly specialized technique practiced 30 feet above the water with heavy tackle for dealing with currents and large gamefish. The best way to take these linesides is to use a bucktail jig either plain or with a squid strip or curly tail sweetener. There is also some live eel fishing, and it is another crabbing spot, which is big in these parts.

"The nearby beach fishing in Ocean City is wide open during the spring and fall striper runs. You can fish around the clock with bottom baits. Locals keep a supply of Gotcha Plugs, MirrOLures, and Rat-L-Traps for when they might run into breaking fish. During summer, when stripers have migrated north and the fishing is more sedate for lesser species, the beach fishing is limited to off hours before 10:00 A.M. and after 5:30 P.M."

CONTACT TIP: Oyster Bay Tackle, Ocean City, (410) 524-3433.

One of the biggest outflows around Indian River draws fish.

11
Indian River Inlet
South of Dewey Beach
Delaware Eastern Shore

BEST MONTHS TO FISH: Stripers—October, November, December, April and May. Other stuff year long except for winter.

RECOMMENDED METHODS: Live eels, live spot, and live mullet (when you can get them). Regulars also use plugs and jigs at times.

FISH YOU CAN EXPECT TO CATCH: Stripers, blues, weakfish, flounder.

HOW TO GET THERE: The inlet is in Delaware Seashore State Park on State Route 1 south of Dewey Beach and about 15 miles north of Ocean City. You drive right over it on Route 1.

In season, stripers are fished here at night with mostly live eels free spooled in the current along with plug fishing. Currents are strong, so it takes a striper sharpie who knows how to work a live eel to get the most out of Indian River Inlet. The best tide is slack tide when fish in the currents are repositioning themselves. Night tides would have an edge anyway but fishing is better during reduced boat traffic—it can be awful weekends and during the day. The best time to avoid the boat traffic is during the deep night and wee hours. Don't hesitate to penetrate the water column with a bucktail jig during times of most intense tidal current. When the water is flying and gamefish are holding in current to forage, get deep and have a place picked out in the rocks to land the buggah.

Just west of the Indian River Bridge on the north side of the inlet there is a popular striper hole with its attendant rips where shore and boat anglers compete with lures and live baits for stripers and blues. The birds often work there during the day and locals know enough to watch it. Indian River Inlet is the best in the region.

CONTACT TIP: Oyster Bay Tackle (mentioned again because they dominate the region), (410) 524-3433.

12

Delaware State Parks
Route 1
Dewey Beach/Indian River, Delaware

BEST MONTHS TO FISH: Stripers—October, November, December, April and May. Other stuff year long except for winter.

RECOMMENDED METHODS: Bottom baits with some artificial lures.

FISH YOU CAN EXPECT TO CATCH: Stripers, blues, weakfish, flounder.

HOW TO GET THERE: The inlet is in Delaware Seashore State Park on State Route 1 south of Dewey Beach and about 15 miles north of Ocean City.

Because of the similarity and proximity of the fishing here, we have again grouped the hot spots as has been the case to the south. However, unlike Ocean City, these areas are more remote and less "citified," enhancing the feel of what surf fishing ought to be like and how it is in most of this book. For one thing we are back to being able to use an ORV, with proper permitting. Parking in season, good anywhere in the park's locations, is five dollars per day but off season and after hours, when it is best for stripers, there is no charge. In Delaware State Parks it is easy to fish the beach either on foot or with an ORV on designated beaches. Be aware of the fragile nature of the dunes and that they are protected by law. Bird nesting areas are also protected during the season. Severe weather conditions can also bring about closures. The beaches largely have a natural drop-off that is not affected by any of the beach replenishment projects.

The first location is just south of the Indian River Inlet on State Route 1 where you can use an ORV. They bottom fish here with all the traditional cut baits or chunks used in the rest of Delmarva. Nearby, and often watched by the Indian River bunch, is what they call the North Pocket off of 3 R's Road Beach.

Fenwick Island Bathhouse, again under park management, is ½ mile north of Fenwick Island and is well known for kingfish, spot and croaker. ORV use with the same permit is allowed.

Cape Henlopen State Park is east of Lewes at the end of Route 9. There are five miles of beach here where Delaware Bay meets the Atlantic. While they surf fish the open beach, there is also a ¼-mile-long Cape Henlopen Fishing Pier. People like to gather at the end, but fish can be anywhere and your chances are better if your bait is the only one around.

Nearby are Roosevelt Inlet, Lewes Canal, and Massey's Landing, located at the end of Long Neck, which is handicapped accessible.

CONTACT TIP: Fenwick Tackle, Fenwick Island, (302) 539-7766.

PENNSYLVANIA

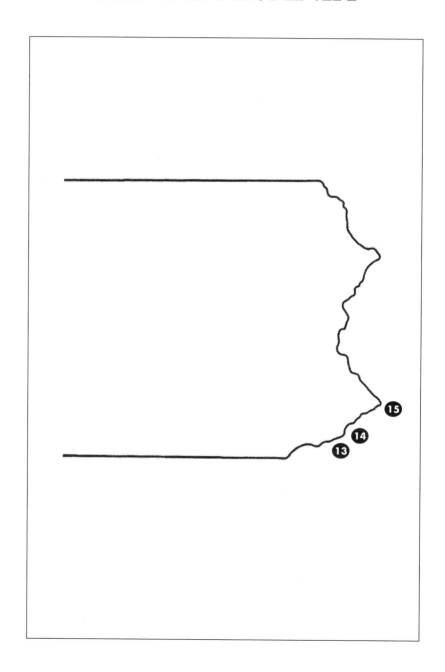

Delaware River Overview

Striped bass are an anadromous species that are native to the region's Atlantic slope rivers occurring within the Delaware River and Susquehanna River drainage. They typically spawn in spring, primarily in the tidal freshwater segments of the Schuylkill and Delaware Rivers. The Delaware River is tidal from the state line upriver beyond Philadelphia to Morrisville, Pennsylvania, some 55 miles. The Schuylkill River is tidal to the Fairmont Dam in Philadelphia. Delaware River juveniles remain in tidal areas for 2 or more years before joining the coastal ocean stock of fish that range from Canada to Florida. Striped bass remain in coastal ocean waters until they mature (males age 2–3 years, females age 4–7) and return to natal rivers in the fall prior to spawning for over-wintering. Then, in spring, they continue their ascent to the uppermost tidal freshwater or brackish water to spawn. Some adults move above the tidal front after or during the spawning period. However, spawning activity or production of young fish appears very limited above the tidal front in this region. Following spawning most adults move downriver and return to the coastal ocean population. Yet, some continue their ascent and very large adults have been caught far above the tidal front, above the confluence with the Lackawaxen River in Pennsylvania, which is 198 miles upriver from the state line.

As the third largest source of Northwest Atlantic migratory stripers, the Delaware River has only recently come into its own as a coastwide stock contributor. Prior to the present, the fishery had been a recruitment failure known to go back as far as the early 60s when extensive testing yielded no apparent striper population in either the estuary or river itself. Hypoxic conditions in and around the city of Philadelphia were so severe that oxygen depletion blocked access by anadromous species to the cleaner foothills waters out of the Catskills. Above Philly, river conditions were suitable but upstream migration was blocked. Environmental improvements during the 80s in the Philadelphia estuary have allayed the formerly impossible situation that prevented upward migration to the spawning grounds. Pollution abatement, which then permitted historically suitable levels of oxygen in the river, had the effect of restoring stripers to an abundance that peaked around 2003/2004.

A creel survey conducted in 2002 showed that over 36,000 striped bass were landed, but not necessarily kept, in the Delaware River. These ranged in size from ten inches to over 30 pounds. Since 1991 over 6,540 stripers up to 48 inches long—over 40 pounds—have been electroshocked and tagged by officials and 21 percent of these have been recaptured and about half released, most by recreational anglers. That same year, 1991, when I was hunting in Hancock, N.Y.—300 miles from tidewater—I knew people who had seen stripers chasing trout in the town's Y-Pool. Recaptures of Delaware River linesides have occurred from North Carolina to Maine. The New Jersey Delaware River record is a 36-pound, 8-ounce lineside taken in 2001. (It won't last.)

Most of the better fishing is around Philadelphia, upstream to Trenton, New Jersey. Even so, stripers are found some years in the upper reaches 17 and 33 miles respectively above Hancock at Cannonsville and Pepacton Reservoirs, over 300 miles from salt water. It has to be a bad joke but it is said they live-line trout in the catching of stripers in some sections of the river. (Don't tell anyone you heard it here.) The linesides are known to frequent the mouths of feeder streams that are known to hold either hatchery or natural trout.

Because four states—Delaware, Pennsylvania New Jersey, and New York—are involved in the river's management, a uniform striper law has been sought to both allay confusion and induce compliance. We hesitate to quote regulations in a lasting treatise like this one, and remind you that the seasons, lines of regulation, size and bag limits are apt to change. We can say that at this writing a freshwater license is required, bait fishing is limited to the use of non-offset circle hooks, and that there are closures to protect spawning activity. Presently, and again it could change, waters from Wilmington to Marcus Hook, the main spawning ground, are catch and release April 1 to May 31.

New to the mix is the fish ladder on the Schuylkill River for mounting the Fairmount Dam in Philadelphia. The first ladder, built in 1979, had only limited use by river-running species. For instance, over 6,400 fish comprised of 25 species counted were serviced by the old fishway in 2004; depending on the year, among these were anywhere from 61 to 130 stripers making it above the dam. A replacement fishway, at a cost of 2.7 million dollars, was constructed in 2008 that is expected to restore striper runs to their prior production levels, adding more migratory stripers to the growing mix of Striper Coast migrants. With acceptable fishways, returns could well be in the thousands per season, which will greatly enhance production. With suitable spawning ground access, it can only get better. As is so often the case elsewhere, boat fishing dominates striper opportunity on the Delaware, but there is some shore fishing, which we will expound upon here where appropriate.

Delaware River regular Mike Spontak with a local fish.
(Courtesy Sabastian Marino)

13

Lower Delaware River
South of Philadelphia
Wilmington, Delaware, to Marcus Hook, Pennsylvania

BEST MONTHS TO FISH FOR STRIPERS: March through June with April and May closure (catch and release).

RECOMMENDED METHODS: Bloodworm and clam bottom baits. Lures and herring chunks late season.

FISH YOU CAN EXPECT TO CATCH: Stripers.

HOW TO GET THERE: West on U.S. Route 322 from New Jersey; south of Philadelphia to the vicinity of the Commodore Barry Bridge.

Exactly where the best fishing might be on so much river is a wild card. The nearer one is fishing to the salt of the Atlantic, the better one's chances are. The most interest in spring spawning stripers is in the vicinity of Commodore Barry and Delaware Memorial Bridges below Philadelphia. There is also a large flat three miles south of Raccoon Creek on the New Jersey side. Bass can be found from this area clear north to above Trenton. Creek mouths are sure to draw feeding stripers, especially after dark. Pennypack Creek, on the west bank, is popular with shore fishermen. It is going to get better once migratory spawning stripers begin running the river now that nearly six miles of river have been opened by the destruction of three dams and the construction of rock ramp fishways. Also, Poquessing Creek is another hot spot within this hot spot. Shore anglers can reach the main river

45

through Hog Island Road via the Island Avenue exit of I–95. Philadelphia National Airport is very close and you can tell who the newbies are because they duck when a plane either lands or takes off. This is a long stretch of shore that accommodates a lot of fishing. Here it is with bottom baits.

A friend of mine who lives on the Delaware River across from Philadelphia says that people would be surprised how good the fishing is in this area. Many anglers think it is only good during April and May with bloodworms, and they abandon the river when summer comes until the next spring. He has had 20 to 30 fish days on lures with fish to 36 inches from June to December. Because these are spawning linesides, every consideration should be given to careful handling and return of these important breeding populations.

CONTACT TIP: Eastern Marine in Newark, Delaware, (302) 737-6603.

14
Schuylkill River
Fairmount Dam
Philadelphia, Pennsylvania

BEST MONTHS TO FISH FOR STRIPERS: March, April, May and June.
RECOMMENDED METHODS: Rat-L-Traps, rubber shads, swimming plugs, bloodworms, and alewife chunks.

FISH YOU CAN EXPECT TO CATCH: Stripers, American white shad, some freshwater species above the dam.

HOW TO GET THERE: From Center City, head west on Kelly Drive. Then at the second light after the Philadelphia Museum of Art, turn left onto Waterworks Drive.

The Schuylkill River has been a victim of river industrialization since the early 19th century. A fishway was constructed in 1979 with the hope of restoring runs of anadromous species, but the business of constructing ladders that the fish will use is an inexact science and few species used it. Likely the new fishway will improve runs to a point where a spot with only marginal qualification like this one could improve enormously.

We include the dam here because fisheries officials electro-shocked a 43-inch striper, probably over 30 pounds, in the fall of 2007. Locals have been catching stripers under the dam for years. One can see that the fish are trying to mount the dam. If they ever do and begin enjoying successful spawning runs, this spot could end up being a major contributor and a five on a scale of five.

Lest you think that the downtown Philadelphia Fairmount Dam is all buttercups and roses, when fishing there at night you had better bring along a National Guard unit for security to ride shotgun on your precious butt for dealing with the potential muggings. Use water-column-penetrating shads and bucktails during the day and stay safe.

CONTACT TIP: Brinkman's Live Bait and Tackle, Philadelphia, (215) 632-0674.

Sabastian Marino with a river bass at Trenton. (Courtesy Sabastian Marino)

15
Upper Delaware River (above tidewater)
Trenton, New Jersey, and Vicinity

BEST MONTHS TO FISH FOR STRIPERS: April, May, and June.

RECOMMENDED METHODS: Rat-L-Traps, rubber shads, swimming plugs, and alewife chunks.

FISH YOU CAN EXPECT TO CATCH: Stripers to 30 pounds, American white shad.

HOW TO GET THERE: Because this a regional collection, getting there depends upon your specific choice.

Upper river fishing begins slightly later than that of the tidal Lower River. Above Philadelphia there is all good water that can be vulnerable some years to an intense snowmelt freshet. High water levels can make the fishing both cloudy and dangerous, as well as more difficult. This spells less risk of a bad trip for those willing to wait for the seasons to adjust. The line where tidewater ends is at Trenton Falls.

Trenton gets the most angling attention, but the bass enjoy a dead shot upstream for hundreds of miles on this spawning run so the fish can be anywhere. The warm-water discharge of the Trenton Power Plant tends to concentrate stripers. Numerous flats get a lot of attention downstream of Trenton, but I would advise anyone wading to be conscious of nuances of the flats along with water levels and river flow rates.

As with the lower river, watch the many creek mouths on both banks for concentrations of bass either feeding on alewives or in their post-spawning period.

CONTACT TIP: H L Live Bait and Tackle, Morrisville, Pennsylvania, (215) 295-1400.

NEW JERSEY

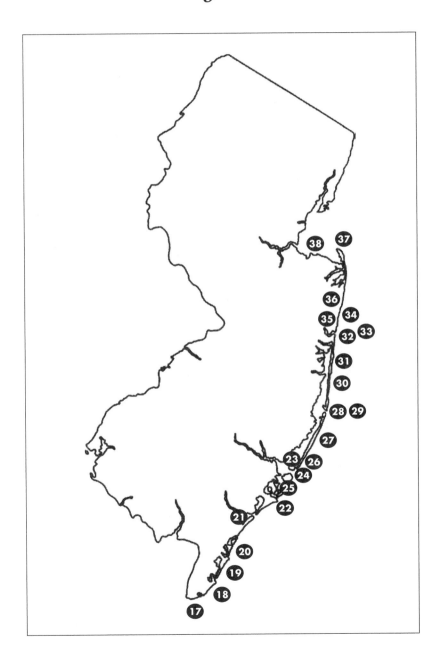

New Jersey

In my early years on Cape Cod I spent many mid-watch hunts for striped bass with what I then called the Jersey bunch. Reminded of the mild cultural differences, because of the way they said things like "the boids is woikin'," I grew to admire and to appreciate their sense of angling purpose. What I remember most about them is that after driving hundreds of miles to a Cape Cod beach, they could never take time out to sleep or eat without feeling a certain guilt. For them, having reached the pinnacle of surfcasting opportunity that the Cape then enjoyed demanded total devotion and allowed no time for creature comforts. One thing I've always known is that there are few casual surfcasters, nor is Jersey a casual surfcasting state. Without real evidence, I think there are more serious surfmen there than any other Striper Coast state.

Lest I be accused of spending more time in the examination of Jersey's people than its fishing, I must note that I was struck by a number of that state's geographical features. It is, above all, a place of countless jetties; so much so that surfcasting has come to mean jetty fishing in the shore-fishing mind there. Another observation I made is that the farther north one went in the Garden State, the better the striper fishing. It is widely believed in the state that being nearer to the Hudson River—a major source of East Coast stripers—can do nothing but help. There are notable climatic differences in New Jersey waters that influence those species found in its surf. For example, you won't find puppy drum north of here, and only an occasional kingfish will visit waters above Long Island, whereas they can be found in nuisance numbers in South Jersey. Unaccountably, porgies—known as scup where I fish—are viewed as an offshore species. And, while I examine predatory species, it is only reasonable to note that forage here is different from that found farther north on the Striper Coast. Anglers who bait fish a spot in Jersey would find no such bait available above Montauk, and only the most astute Rhode Island observer would even be conscious of a fall mullet run in his state, while it is a major natural event in New Jersey. Crabs and clams are popular striper bait in South Jersey, yet never used for linesides in Massachusetts or Rhode Island.

There is also a greater transition from bait fishing to lure fishing in New Jersey, clear evidence of some sort of departure that so dominates the waters to the south. In truth, this trend to greater use of artificials continues as we travel north. Not that bait fishing ever leaves the arsenal entirely, but the trend is there.

Lastly, I must acknowledge that the per capita number of surf fishermen in this state is surely the largest of any state on the Striper Coast. On Thanksgiving morning of '91—and this is a holiday celebrated by nearly all Americans, a day that custom and tradition acknowledge as one of the most significant family holidays of the year—there was no room to stand or fish among the 3,000-plus surfcasters lined up on Island Beach . . . at (are you ready?) 4:00 A.M.

(Courtesy Patrick O'Donnell)

NUANCES OF JETTIES

With so much of the fishing in New Jersey and Long Island being done from jetties, it might be a good idea to talk about the nuances of jetty fishing in this one discussion to serve forthcoming jetty-specific hot spots.

Much of traditional jetty fishing is no longer practical because in order to deal with a big bass it is necessary to use a a gaff to subdue it. With catch-and-release fishing so much in vogue, it makes no sense to risk wounding a fish that you do not plan to keep. The regulars that I know prefer a smaller fish on that rare occasion that they might keep one for the table. Trying to beach a big fish from a difficult jetty is dangerous, and you'll probably kill the fish from exhaustion even if you make it. Nonetheless, if a person is going to fish from a jetty a long-handled gaff is necessary—probably six or eight feet long is sufficient. We always covered the gaff point with a section of rubber hose for safety. I knew one surfcaster who painted a white stripe on the side of the gaff away from the hook so that he always knew where it was facing in the dark. Also, stuck in the jetty rocks, one can hang on to it for support in rough water. It is a good idea to have a section of rope to tie onto a fish while you climb back out from the jetty base that only moments ago nearly killed you. Once upon top, you can retrieve your fish with the rope.

Damage from storms over the years makes jetties variable in protection, danger, and how they influence the fishing. Many are nothing more than small rock piles in decline while others are new and quite user friendly. They face directly into the ocean, so most waves come in head-on. You're almost always fishing the end, so you get to stare down some pretty awesome combers. People get hurt more on jetties than any situation that I can think of in surfcasting. With thousands of hours on a multitude of jetties, many of us have been knocked down too many times to count. You risk being covered by green water and once lifted you have no way of knowing where or when you are coming down.

When you see a big wave coming that you know is going to hit you, stand sideways. Never face it squarely. Lean into it and use your rod as a support if necessary. On a large jetty, two men can link up with their rods and get four-legged support against a heavy sea. Never try to run from a wave . . . it will catch you from behind and you may get a ride you won't forget. When it gets that bad know when to get out. In addition, keep an eye peeled on your exit route or the way off could be blocked by a building sea.

Etiquette and cooperation are a must, and all anglers need to be fishing in similar styles. One person cannot be bottom fishing and another plugging where you tangle with one another. Utilizing similar weighted offerings or the same type of lure if drifting with the current enhances compatibility. Cooperative rotations should be initiated. Be aware of someone fighting a fish and watch what's going on before making a cast. No lights should be shone on the water as some guys are very touchy about that.

Good footwear is critical. Cleats or spikes that cover the sole and heel of your boot foot, or felt bottoms on some jetty surfaces, work well. One-inch #14 metal screws set in a neoprene sole are sometimes used, and I have seen golf cleats set in a rubber overshoe work. On the tougher, greasier rock piles, Korkers are the safest choice. Waders work in many places. Often in my buggy fishing, I have relied upon hip boots and oilskin pants. During snotty nights, add an oilskin top. Also, remember that wool clothing will keep you warm when wet.

Rats live down in the rocks of most jetties and they commonly raid lunches or feast upon a fish carelessly left only a few feet away. (Don't shoot them as the salt water is bad for your sidearm.)

COURTESY: StriperSurf forum discussion, Ask Frank Daignault.

16
New Jersey Saltwater Fishing Piers

BEST MONTHS TO FISH: March through December.

RECOMMENDED METHODS: Bottom baits.

FISH YOU CAN EXPECT TO CATCH: All indigenous species—bass, blues, porgy, king fish, weakfish.

HOW TO GET THERE: Locations below.

Atlantic County
Edward Ungenerous Fishing Pier
Between Somers Point and Longport—Broad Thoroughfare
    off Great Egg Harbor Bay

Old Brigantine Bridge
Brigantine across Absecon Inlet
From Harrah's Marina—Absecon Inlet

Margate Fishing Pier
The Angler's Club
Margate City—oceanfront

Ventnor City Fishing Pier
Cambridge Avenue and the Boardwalk, Ventnor City—
    oceanfront
Fee information is available by calling (609) 823-7944

Cape May County
Ocean City Fishing Club
14th and Boardwalk, Ocean City—oceanfront
(609) 398-9800

Monmouth County
Keansburg Fishing Pier
Keansburg—Raritan Bay
(732) 495-8842

Keyport Fishing Pier
Keyport—Raritan Bay

Ocean County
Beach Haven Pier
Beach Haven
2nd Street and the bay—Barnegat Bay

Seaside Heights Fishing Pier
Casino Pier
Seaside Heights—oceanfront

Seaside Heights
two piers—Barnegat Bay
(Courtesy: N.J. Division of Fish and Wildlife)

17
Cape May Point
Cape May, New Jersey

BEST MONTHS TO FISH: April through December.

RECOMMENDED METHODS: Lures and baits.

FISH YOU CAN EXPECT TO CATCH: Stripers, bluefish, weakfish, kingfish, flounder, and tautog.

HOW TO GET THERE: At the end of the Garden State Parkway, go straight south over the bridge into town. It's a direct run. Follow the signs to Cape May Point State Park from the Garden State Parkway.

In the vicinity of Cape May Point and Lighthouse, there are eight jetties, any of which can produce suitable fishing for just about every species listed for this area. Farther west, there is another, less popular, group of jetties. Those fishing "the point" like to see a northeast wind, because it piles up water, bait, and gamefish along this part of the shore. Tidewise, there are individual preferences, but most to whom I spoke said they liked the outgoing tide. No doubt, this preference takes into account that during a moon tide a nor'easter will cover most of the jetties with dangerous foam, making it about impossible to fish many of them. Outgoing tides are safe, as conditions are unlikely to get worse.

The bathing beach section is closed to fishing during any time when the life guards are on duty, usually 10:00 A.M. to 5:00 P.M. Because there is no bathing at the sunken ship area, you can fish there at any time.

Cape May Inlet, which is guarded on both shores by fishable jetties, is probably the best of it, but the military keeps both sides under tight control. The south jetty is accessible only to Coast Guard personnel, and the north is closed to vehicles unless the owner has a military I.D. (which includes military retirees and those with a red Reserve card). Diehards walk the 2 miles when striper fishing heats up—which can be anytime, but more likely late fall. I'm told that the north jetty is worth the walk.

There is some fly fishing in the sod banks to the east of the Garden State before Cape May by taking a left onto North Wildwood Boulevard where the water is a lot warmer in springtime. In the back they access Nummy Island at North Wildwood and Mill Creek near the toll bridge.

Methods vary more widely here because of the variety of species involved; thus, details for each of the less glamorous species are being bypassed to say more about stripers. Early season, when the water is cold, fishing begins with bottom baits until the water temperature reaches 50 degrees, then lure fishing kicks in. Plug fishing is just as popular here as elsewhere and remains the center of interest. However, the fall mullet run, starting in September, finds many anglers using actual mullet or plug imitations. Live eels are another choice that is distinctive in that the smaller "whip" eels, rated at thirteen to the pound, are often used with light tackle. At an average of an ounce and a quarter each, these small baits are drifted along the jetty edges.

CONTACT TIP: Inquire about Cape May at Rodia's Bait and Tackle, Cape May, (609) 886-0505.

18
Hereford Inlet
North Wildwood, New Jersey

BEST MONTHS TO FISH: April through December.

RECOMMENDED METHODS: Lures and baits, fly fishing in the back.

FISH YOU CAN EXPECT TO CATCH: Stripers, bluefish, weakfish, kingfish, flounder.

HOW TO GET THERE: Take Garden State Parkway exit 4 to Route 147 east, North Wildwood Boulevard. Three miles east on the boulevard, take a left onto Ocean Drive if you want to fish the back.

Two of the eight jetties on the south side of Hereford Inlet are sanded in, but the others provide opportunities for all species in season. Most popular are the Surf Avenue and New York Avenue jetties. As with Cape May, northeast winds are popular, and slack tides at both ends seem to be what anglers seek. The exception seems to be flounder fishermen, who like high tides. Better opportunities for kingfish, I'm told, are in the back, the more estuarine part of the inlet; regulars use bloodworms or shrimp on the bottom. Crossing the two ocean bridges, drive north to the back, where there are wadable marsh areas; it is possible to plug light gear or fly fish during the night for school striper fishing, which is mostly catch-and-release fishing but there is always a chance for a keeper. While there are two main channels at this writing, the inlet is largely sanded in and doesn't exchange as much water as many other inlets on this coast.

CONTACT TIP: Gibson's Tackle, Sea Isle City, (609) 263-6540.

19
Townsend's Inlet
Sea Isle City and Avalon, New Jersey

BEST MONTHS TO FISH: April through December, but fall is best.

RECOMMENDED METHODS: Big plugs, rigged eels, fly fishing, and live baits that represent what is available—mullet, eels, and pogies.

FISH YOU CAN EXPECT TO CATCH: Stripers, blues, kingfish, fluke, and blackfish.

HOW TO GET THERE: From the Garden State Parkway, take exit 13 to Avalon, then go north on Ocean Drive for two miles. For a north bank approach take exit 17 for Sea Isle City, then right onto Landis Avenue on the north bank.

They say there is no favored side to Townsend's Inlet, where anglers line up to cash in on the currents flowing from behind the barrier beach. Knowing what I know about inlets, I would favor the drop. Though there are no actual inlet jetties, there is a rockline on the south side. There are, however, some true jetties on the south side in Avalon. The Eighth Street jetty is popular, because it is both long and easy going with cement filling the cracks. On some evenings or early dawns, the fishermen lined up here look like a fence line from a distance.

Currents are strong at the inlet itself with some anglers preferring an hour each side of the slack in tide. Falling tides should be better than the rise, but whenever water isn't suitable at the inlet, it is possible to work the many jetties. As in much of South Jersey, when stripers and blues are slow during the summer, they are compensated for by the other, less glamorous, species. There is good blackfishing (tog) under the bridge on the south side. As the approaches are township land, there are no access problems, but day parking in summer can be tough. All of this area is highly accessible by car, but after September 15 you can use a buggy.

There are lights on the north end of the bridge where there seems to be the most current. I would advise anyone there at night to check out the shadows cast by the combination of bridge and lights for stripers holding, facing the current. These will appear as dark on gray fish forms, and a bucktail jig is the best way to deal with this prime situation.

Of the two major current sources, the one coming from the southwest is the stronger over the northeast flow. Just how much this influences the fishing as to which end of the bridge is better would require further study. Learning could be a very interesting experience.

Fishing in the back has to be a pushover. The best approach would be flats wading with a fly rod or light spinning after dark. I would think that boat traffic would be a determinant, so you would be advised to pick a night when boaters sleep.

CONTACT TIP: Call Fin-Atics, Ocean City, (609) 398-2248.

Day fishing at Corsons.

20

Corson's Inlet (Strathmere Inlet)
Strathmere/Ocean City, New Jersey

BEST MONTHS TO FISH: April through December; fall is best.

RECOMMENDED METHODS: Big plugs, rigged eels, fly fishing, and bottom baits that represent what is available—mullet and pogies.

FISH YOU CAN EXPECT TO CATCH: Stripers, blues, kingfish, fluke, and blackfish.

HOW TO GET THERE: From the Garden State Parkway take the Ocean City exit (25) to Roosevelt Boulevard then right or south onto Central and follow the signs to Corsons Inlet State Park.

There is a lot of access here because of the state park, what with the fishing pier and the inlet itself. Another plus is that there is ample parking so there are no hassles. The inlet is really two inlets that meet in the back just before dumping into the open sea. The sea side is loaded with shallow bars that would require some intimacy for a wading surfcaster to wade safely. At least do it on the drop in tide for the first time, as that is safer.

This is a popular daytime spot for easy-to-catch eating fish like weaks, kings, and fluke. Still, and don't hold me to the year, a shore fisherman around 2002 beached a 55-pound striper in the daylight in mid-summer; you never know. There is also a fishing pier in Ocean City at 14th and Boardwalk.

As is the case with so many of these inlets that exchange water with the back, wading the marsh trenches in the deep night fly fishing would have to support a great fishery with light tackle.

This is a great place for an ORV or beach-buggy in the non-bathing period in spring and fall. Vehicular over-sand use is not permitted May 15 to September 15. There is a $50 fee for the annual permit. (See "Usual and Customary Requirements for an Over-Sand Vehicle.")

There are eight or nine jetties at the north end of this seven or eight miles of beach approaching Egg Harbor that get plenty of attention from local surfcasters once the bathing season ends and ORVs are back into use.

CONTACT TIP: Tim's Tackle Box, Ocean City, (609) 399-0323.

21
Great Egg Harbor
North of Ocean City, New Jersey

BEST MONTHS TO FISH: April through December.

RECOMMENDED METHODS: Light tackle with artificials and fly fishing.

FISH YOU CAN EXPECT TO CATCH: Stripers, blues.

HOW TO GET THERE: From the south take the Ocean City exit from the Garden State Parkway to Route 52, Stainton Memorial Causeway, then right onto Bay Avenue. From the north take the Longport Road, 152. Using either approach, you'll go over the water in four places: Stainton Causeway, Ocean City Boulevard and Somers Point Boulevard in two places

We rate this spot low because it is a commando job location. What I mean by that is that without a public access, you have to paint your face and crawl around private property and non-owned property where locals exercise their proprietary rights by calling the cops or having your vehicle towed. There is a great rip at the Egg Harbor Inlet but the challenge is not in the fish but in the fishing. The south edge of the inlet is barry and there is more current on the north edge from the Longport approach. I just don't know if you can get in there. It is also a regional location rather than a specific set of stones or particular beach—almost a non-spot for anyone looking for a specific location.

Your best chance is to fish the nooks and crannies in the back parts of the harbor when things are socially/humanly slower in the off season wherever you can pull off with your vehicle and get in the quiet marshes where stripers really live. Your Navy SEAL training will come in handy. But, it is places like these that few others know the ropes and where you—if you keep your mouth shut—can turn your grandchildren into striper legends. Often hot spots like this one are the jewels of the Striper Coast.

CONTACT TIP: One Stop Bait and Tackle, Atlantic City, (609) 348-9450.

22
Absecon Inlet Plus
Atlantic City, New Jersey

BEST MONTHS TO FISH: May through December.

RECOMMENDED METHODS: Plugs, fly fishing, rigged eels, live eels, and free swimming live baits when available.

FISH YOU CAN EXPECT TO CATCH: Stripers and bluefish.

HOW TO GET THERE: Follow the Atlantic City Expressway right into Atlantic City, then take Atlantic Avenue to a right onto New Hampshire; take a left two blocks down onto Oriental, which leads to the inlet and the T-jetty.

The first four jetties on the south side of Absecon Inlet, and there are eight in all, are a popular collection of jetties right in Atlantic City that produce stripers on a regular basis. Naturally, those nearest the inlet enjoy better current. The T-jetty, which borders the inlet, is used regularly and is flat and easy. Keep in mind that flow in this area causes the north sides of rock piles to be deeper. While both sides of the jetty on the Brigantine or north side of the inlet are fished, the north side seems to have an edge in spite of better currents on the south. This reputation may have advanced itself during the fall migration when fish came down the beach from the north. Being that they are surfcasters, who knows what is in their heads.

Back in Atlantic City, and for obvious reasons we are obliged to mention this, the Vermont Avenue jetty (south side) is the spot where Albert McReynolds landed the 78½-pound striper in the early '80s for an All-Tackle World Record that still holds at this writing. His accomplishment played some part in the rating of this area. However, the intense tourism of summer, coupled with crowds of transient people of dubious intent, raised the specter of security issues, which bring into question the wisdom of summer fishing for the lone surfcaster in the deep of night. This is, after all, the city. No doubt some regulars are willing to put a few plugs in their bag and a lot of grenades along with a spare clip.

CONTACT TIP: Offshore Enterprises Bait and Tackle, Atlantic City, (609) 345-9099.

The flats of Graveling Point have good fly fishing for everything at night.

23

Graveling Point (Radio Road approach)
Great Bay
South of West Tuckerton Landing
(Little Egg Harbor), New Jersey

BEST MONTHS TO FISH: April through December.

RECOMMENDED METHODS: Bait fishing, "99 percent" say the bait and tackle shops, fly fishing says Frank, but both are safe.

FISH YOU CAN EXPECT TO CATCH: Stripers and bluefish, weakfish, fluke, and tautog.

HOW TO GET THERE: From the north take Forge Road to the southeast right after Stafford Forge. From the south leave the Garden State Parkway at Bass River and go east on Route 9 to West Tuckerton Landing, also known locally as Little Egg Harbor. From there go south on Radio Road from West Tuckerton Landing to land's end.

This is another regional collection of spots that enjoys the protection of being in the back while providing excellent light tackle fishing, whether with light spinning or fly rod. Served by Scott's Bait and Tackle in Little Egg Harbor, this shore-based location offers a couple of spots for anglers in waders—Graveling Point and Mystic Beach, which are adjacent at the end of Radio Road. While it is a suitable spot for stripers and other species, the reputation of this area for being schoolie country kind of lowers it. Still, as with anywhere else on the Striper Coast, they have their keepers too. Locals say that at least one "fifty" comes from the Mullica River's influence each season. One reason why the fishing holds up is due to the influences of the Mullica River, which is just west of both spots. The folks I contacted swore that it was all bait fishing, but anyone can see that it would be a cinch to fly fish all of this after dark. Who knows, maybe they say that to sell more bait.

CONTACT TIP: Absecon Bay Sportsman Center, Absecon Bay, (609) 484-0409 or (800) 352-2524.

24

Mystic Islands
Great Bay
South of West Tuckerton Landing
(Little Egg Harbor), New Jersey

BEST MONTHS TO FISH: April through December.

RECOMMENDED METHODS: Bait fishing, "99 percent" say the bait and tackle shops, fly fishing.

FISH YOU CAN EXPECT TO CATCH: Stripers, bluefish, weakfish, fluke, and tautog.

HOW TO GET THERE: Only 200 yards east of Radio Road in Little Egg Harbor is Great Bay Boulevard. Follow Great Bay Boulevard south and pick up the spots until you reach land's end.

Fifth Bridge, which is the last bridge you drive over before reaching the end of the island, is one of the spots favored for shore fishing. For one thing, regardless of tide, the currents never quit because water is always flowing from one side or the other of the island. There are several outflows that meet the open water of Great Bay on each side of the main Mystic Island, which would have to draw fish because of their currents.

Two other spots, the end of the boulevard and South Green Street, are also good for shore fishing the island's end. Like the area near the Mullica River, Spot 22, we are not talking monster fish here but the wild cards in ocean fishing are still being dealt. If I lived around there I might score the Mystic

Islands as a half a fish better than Graveling Point because it is closer to open water.

CONTACT TIP: Scott's Bait and Tackle, Bradley Beach, (609) 296-1300.

The sandy shoreline of Brigantine makes landing a cow easier.

25
Brigantine Inlet
Brigantine, New Jersey

BEST MONTHS TO FISH: April through December.

RECOMMENDED METHODS: Plugs, eels, bottom baits, and fly fishing.

73

FISH YOU CAN EXPECT TO CATCH: Stripers, bluefish, weakfish, kingfish, and flounder.

HOW TO GET THERE: Follow the Atlantic City Expressway into Atlantic City, then go left onto Atlantic Avenue. Only ¼ mile north, take a left onto Martin Luther King Boulevard and stay on it until you cross Absecon Boulevard to Huron Avenue. Continue a half mile to Brigantine Boulevard, Route 87 (County Route 638), which takes you over water into Brigantine, and follow signs to Brigantine. Once in town go northbound on East Brigantine Avenue to where civilization ends and the dunes begin. About a three-mile dune road leads to the inlet.

The long, slow curve of Brigantine Inlet is all sand. Because there are no jetties, bottom sand shifts as the product of a season's winds and currents, and it is a perfect spot for reading the many shallow sloughs and holes that develop there. Again, northeast winds are popular, even though they are in your face here, and dropping tides seem to draw available fish to these shallows. It may be more important to fish at night here, however, because stripers are often reluctant to risk shallow water without the cover of darkness. The premise that night fishing is basic to surf fishing is all the more important in shallow locations like this one. Also, don't hesitate to fly fish the back—at night.

The distance from hard top to inlet is about ¾ of a mile, and the town does issue permits to drive the beach with a buggy. Follow the rules, and avoid shining your headlights on the water wherever you are going to fish. There are some who would put a contract out on me for divulging this spot.

CONTACT TIP: Rip Tide Bait and Tackle, Brigantine, (609) 264-0440.

26
Beach Haven Inlet (Hole Gate)
Long Beach Island
Beach Haven, New Jersey

BEST MONTHS TO FISH: April through December.

RECOMMENDED METHODS: Lures and baits, some fly fishing.

FISH YOU CAN EXPECT TO CATCH: Stripers, bluefish, weaks, kingfish, and flounder.

HOW TO GET THERE: Take exit 63 off the Garden State Parkway, then go east on Route 72 to Ship Bottom. Turn right (south) onto Long Beach Boulevard and proceed about 10 miles where you'll find the inlet. It is about a four-mile beach run to the inlet. (An over-sand vehicle is helpful after September 15.)

The inlet at Beach Haven is one of the region's best shore fishing hot spots. While any of the last 3 miles will produce all species, the nearer you go to the end, with its currents, the better your chances are of finding suitable fishing. With so much flow from Little Egg Harbor, it is not necessary to restrict your fishing to any particular tide. Regulars all claim that they do as well on the upcoming water as on the drop. As with the more southerly Jersey areas, the northeaster is a popular wind, and the nor'wester helps the cast when the angle of this beach is considered. A popular way to fish stripers, blues, and weaks here is to utilize a mullet rig bottom fishing. This is a pin harness with a small cork float that lifts the bait off the bottom to avoid scavengers. Early in the season, before mullet present themselves, chunks—bunker or mackerel—can be used on the bottom.

Methods, hook size, bait, time of day, and season determine what species are likely, though I admit to frequent surprises. Small offers take fluke, kingfish, and smaller weaks; big plugs or eels cull out small stuff in favor of bigger stripers when they are around, and they are most often around in the fall. Don't overlook the more protected back estuary if you like fly fishing. There are several points on the north side of this peninsula, in the back, where the current picks up because of narrows that should always be checked out if the inlet itself is not productive. A prominent point, about a half mile short of the inlet, is very promising.

With the required town permit, beach buggies may be used starting September 15. Locals wait for that date because it enables them to drive the last ½ mile to the inlet until May 15. They walk it in warmer months.

CONTACT TIP: Grucella Bait and Tackle, Long Beach, (609) 494-5739.

27
Long Beach Island
New Jersey

BEST MONTHS TO FISH: April through December, but fall is best.
RECOMMENDED METHODS: Lures and baits.
FISH YOU CAN EXPECT TO CATCH: Stripers, bluefish, weaks, kingfish, and flounder.

HOW TO GET THERE: Take exit 63 off the Garden State Parkway, then go east on Route 72 to Ship Bottom.

This entire 12-mile stretch entertains migrating schools of gamefish. Because of the shore road here, it is possible to drive the entire island to locate schools of fish feeding along the shore. The whole island is laced with jetties, but these are low and unsuitable for walking or crawling, as they often flood; however, they still draw migrants at both ends of the season because of the cover they offer.

Bluefish are the most likely to be seen, but by November expect schools of bass as well, which can last late into December. A widely held belief is that the later it is in the season, the more likely one is to find action in the daytime. Still, if linesides are around, and you can take the water temperatures, night remains prime. Plugs and lures are best in the fall because of the mobility that goes with using them. It should be noted that after Labor Day it is possible to acquire a beach-buggy permit (about $60) for all the towns from Harvey Cedars south.

CONTACT TIP: Bruce and Pat's, Surf City, (609) 494-2333.

28
Barnegat Inlet South Jetty
Barnegat Light, North of Long Beach Park
New Jersey

BEST MONTHS TO FISH: April through December.
RECOMMENDED METHODS: Lures and baits.

Jetties, like Barnegat, provide access to deep-water currents.
(Courtesy Patrick O'Donnell)

FISH YOU CAN EXPECT TO CATCH: Stripers, bluefish, weaks, kingfish, flounder, and blackfish.

HOW TO GET THERE: Take exit 63 off the Garden State Parkway, then go east on Route 72 to Ship Bottom. Take a left (north) onto Long Beach Boulevard then left onto Broadway and follow it for 8-plus miles to Barnegat Light.

Three years in the making, the new 3,224-foot-long South Jetty was completed in 1992. It has turned out to be a great place from which to fish with fewer of the issues often found in rugged, beat-up jetties. It is so new, and so flat, that you don't need cleats.

There is even a handrail for the first 1,000 feet. This is all public property and there are no parking hassles.

Opinions about this spot were beginning to emerge just as I wrote this: The end of the jetty is preferred; the dropping tide is best, particularly low slack when big stripers shift positions. Weakfish are more likely on the south, or outside of the rocks, stripers more likely on the north, or inside, where the serious currents are. When fishing for blackfish, remember that they are more likely to be found at the jetty base near the rocks. Outside of the mullet season, deadly bait for bass are calico crabs or soft shedder blue claws; split the big ones to create a scent. This spot is among the best-in-state, with anglers lined up on both sides of Barnegat Inlet.

CONTACT TIP: Barnegat Light Bait and Tackle, Barnegat Light, (609) 494-4566.

29
Barnegat Inlet North Jetty
Island Beach State Park
South of South Seaside Park, New Jersey

BEST MONTHS TO FISH: May, June; September through December.

RECOMMENDED METHODS: Live bait and swimming plugs.

FISH YOU CAN EXPECT TO CATCH: Stripers, bluefish, weakfish, fluke, and blackfish.

HOW TO GET THERE: Take exit 82 off the Garden State Parkway, then Route 37 east to Tom's River and Seaside Heights.

The best striper fishing is at both ends of the season.

Follow signs to Island Beach and drive south the entire 11½-mile length of this barrier beach island to arrive at Barnegat Inlet.

It is 1½ miles on foot from the southernmost parking area to the jetty. Stretching southeast from the beach, the jetty is over 200 yards long. It can be wet (depending on the wind) and spikes or Korkers are needed along with full foul-weather suiting. The dropping tide is popular here along the inlet side of the jetty. When fishing the ocean side of the jetty, however, an incoming tide is preferred. There is an excellent corner known as "The Pocket" where jetty joins beach that locals run to when the wind is north or nor'east. The clams get washed up there and the bass go nuts. I would rate The Pocket a five fish rating when this happens.

Best striper fishing is at both ends of the season, with July and August avoided by most. As with all of Jersey, the September mullet run triggers a fall heat-up of stripers, blues, and weakfish. Notwithstanding, there is some commercial mullet netting activity that can hinder your fishing. Note that fluke and, to some degree, weakfish augment summer fishing enough to fill out the calendar.

Over-sand vehicles are commonly used to cover the last stretch from the parking lot. A permit is required, along with the usual equipment: jack, shovel, board, air gauge, tow rope. There are three-day permits for those visiting for $50 and an annual permit, which costs $195 at this writing.

CONTACT TIP: The Hook House, Toms River, (908) 270-3856.

30

Sedge Island
Barnegat Bay
Island Beach State Park
South of South Seaside Park, New Jersey

BEST MONTHS TO FISH: Late April through December.

RECOMMENDED METHODS: Bucktails, small plugs, and fly fishing.

FISH YOU CAN EXPECT TO CATCH: Stripers, bluefish, weakfish, and fluke.

HOW TO GET THERE: Take exit 82 off the Garden State Parkway, then Route 37 east to Tom's River and Seaside Heights. Follow signs to Island Beach and proceed south to Barnegat Inlet.

The outgoing tide is best at the Sedges.

This protected estuarine spot is in the back of the last parking area, but access from there is difficult. Most people get to "the Sedge" by walking from the inlet toward the back bay. Less of a walk than to the North Jetty, what anglers call "Sedge Island" is really not the island itself but a strip of land toward the island in the rip between the barrier beach and island. The narrow passage of water between the barrier and the island is the big appeal. The outgoing tide is best. During the higher stages of tide, there is also some excellent flats-wading where plugs or flies can be used in the deep of night. Kayakers love it back there. Because of its protected nature, this spot is a lifesaver when the front beach is getting a pasting from a storm. When baitfishing for blackfish, use sand crabs and pick the rocky areas.

CONTACT TIP: Grumpy's Bait and Tackle, Toms River, (732) 830-1900.

31

Island Beach
Island Beach State Park (IBSP)
South of South Seaside Park, New Jersey

BEST MONTHS TO FISH: May and June, and September through December.

RECOMMENDED METHODS: Bottom baits, clams are popular, all plugs, and lures.

FISH YOU CAN EXPECT TO CATCH: Stripers, bluefish, weakfish, fluke, and blackfish.

Island Beach, the crown jewel of Jersey. (Courtesy Patrick O'Donnell)

HOW TO GET THERE: Take exit 82 off the Garden State Parkway, then Route 37 east to Tom's River then Seaside Heights. Follow signs right or south to Island Beach State Park.

The beach fishing portion of the whole 10 miles of Island Beach State Park can be fished best when an over-sand vehicle is used. That is not to say that a buggy is required, because a car can be utilized on the road paralleling the beach, but a buggy enables a surfcaster to view the entire waterline in spring and fall and much of it during the summer. Also, one can make the most of mobility by utilizing plugs or lures. Fall fishing is what Jersey hungries all wait for. Here are some details on the beach.

(Courtesy Patrick O'Donnell)

The bathing pavilions take up about the first ¾ of a mile of beach. Here beach-buggy use is limited from mid-May to the first week of October. Otherwise it is all walk-on for fishing during summer, which is limited to nights or when the lifeguards are not on duty. This early, the north end of the bathing beach is still good fishing when things are quiet. There is usually a good-looking slough between the first and second bathing beaches.

The parking areas are numbered south of the bathing beaches starting with A2. (Don't ask about A1.) The numbers rise as one travels south. From here on the walk is pretty easy and there are some good holes clear to A7, known as the "Fisherman's Walkway." This is also the location of the second access road

Aerial view of North Jetty Inlet. (Courtesy Bob Ragati)

right after an air-up station for buggies at A6. There is also a parking lot there that holds around 30 cars, which fills up early during summer because of a convenient long boardwalk out to the beach, or it will fill early in fall if the blitz is on. In the back, on the bay side, they fly fish a spot called Tices Shoal more during the off season when it's all fishing and the bathers are gone and the boaters are scraping their hulls.

Everything south of A7 is the southern natural area. From A10 to A18 the hike over the dunes is a little farther (which could change) but many surfcasters think it is worthwhile. They call A12/A13 the "Judges Shack," which is an old fishing shack on top of the dunes. The structure is not that remarkable, but decent

Aerial view looking south on IBSP. (Courtesy Bob Ragati)

stripers come out of there every year and it is important enough to have a landmark to go by. The rocket scientist who does the counting around here missed on A16, which is the Interpretive Center and used to be a Coast Guard Station. Parking lots from A18 to A23 hold more cars than those mentioned earlier at the north and are an easier walk over the dunes. A21 has the "Million Dollar Outhouse" built a couple of years ago that is solar and wind powered. (Another don't ask.) In this same A21 they launch a lot of yaks in the back for use at the Sedge Islands (see above). The paved road ends at A23, 1½ miles from the north jetty of Barnegat Inlet—a long walk. Fall to spring, however, that is all buggy drivable with the beach permit.

Northern Area: Just inside the gate on the left is Two Bit Road, a short shell-covered trail that ends at a parking area for maybe 10 or so cars. When you see the Porta-Potty, you are there. It is a short walk over the dunes, nice deep water, usually with cuts, and clam beds. They do well there and you don't need a buggy. About ½ mile further down the paved road is the "Maintenance Building" sometimes referred to as "110," named for the former Coast Guard station that occupies it. There is parking across the road for about 15–20 cars. A longer trail over the dunes leads to the beach and is another good spot for those that don't mind the travel. About a ¾-mile walk further south of that is the "Governor's Mansion." There is no parking at all there but good fishing. One mile south of the mansion is Gillikens, the first buggy access road. If you have a buggy pass, you can park on the beach and walk north, and there is also some good fishing there. Gillikens is very popular and it can be really good or totally frustrating. There is usually some good structure there, with deep troughs behind the bars, great cuts in the bars, and clam beds that seem to hold the stripers. Gillikens extends to the "Recreation Area," which is closed to buggies from mid-May until the beginning of October. The thing that attracts many to the northern area is it's all fishing—no bonfires, no kids throwing Frisbees, no bathers in the summer. Generally, the water to the north is deeper than the water to the south. As one might expect, there is variability in the productivity of this long beach. The bars, sloughs, and holes are so variable that trying to rate stretches when they are always changing is futile. It is thus a case of a surfcaster's beach-reading ability to decipher the best fishing as well as what people say.

Life is good. (Courtesy Patrick O'Donnell)

For instance, everybody coughs when you ask about Gillikens north of the bathing beach or recreation area; now why would they do that? It is a short walk over the dunes to some of the deepest water around, which holds some attractive structure and clam beds that stripers get horsed over year long. The high-liner contact that helped me so much here sometimes kills them there.

The northern area is probably the most productive part of IBSP, from the sign "No Buggies Beyond this Point" north to the Old Life Saving Station and the Governor's Mansion. Deep water is the draw. The beach permit, the same one used for the north jetty of Barnegat, is $195 and they offer a 3-day for $50. As with all fees, they are likely to rise.

CONTACT TIP: Grumpy's Tackle, Tom's River, (732) 830-1900. IBSP Park Headquarters, (732) 793-0506.

Here are the mandatory requirements for beach driving specific to IBSP:
- Fishing equipment for each person over the age of 12
- Tire pressure gauge
- Full-sized spare tire
- Workable jack
- Support board ¾ inch × 12 × 12 minimum
- Shovel, not a plastic toy
- Flashlight
- Fire extinguisher
- Auto first-aid kit
- Tow chain or snatch line
- Litter/trash bag for carry on/carry out
- Minimum of ¾ tank of fuel

Rules for Beach use:
- Stay off the dunes and vegetation.
- Observe 10 mph speed limit.
- Drivers yield to the right.
- No alcoholic beverages.
- No camping.
- Pets must be leashed, and bring at least a gallon of water for the dog.
- You must be actively fishing.
- During summer pay close attention to sunbathers, kids, dogs, and other 4 × 4s.

32

Point Pleasant Canal
Point Pleasant, New Jersey

BEST MONTHS TO FISH: May through October.

RECOMMENDED METHODS: Alewives and lures.

FISH YOU CAN EXPECT TO CATCH: Stripers.

HOW TO GET THERE: Take Garden State Parkway to exit 91, Burnt Tavern Road east. Just before the Lovelandtown Bridge, with it in sight, take the last right and park just beyond the State Police Marine Barracks near a small cove. On the east side of the canal go right on over the bridge to a traffic light on Bay Avenue where you take a right that will lead you directly to the end. It looks built up but fishing access is guaranteed.

The canal, about 1½ miles long and roughly 100 yards wide, connects the Manasquan River to Upper Barnegat Bay. There are two good spots on the canal—one on the west and another on the east, but both are at the south end of the canal. The first one you come to, on the west, you'll see that they launch boats in the cove, and there is plenty of current flowing under the bridge. There is a three-foot chain-link fence—they don't want you to fall in—on most of the canal, so have either a net or gaff to deal with frisky gamefish. Across the canal, following to the end of Bay Avenue, there is a condo complex with plenty of parking that can scare you if you are used to getting kicked out of spots, but don't worry about that. When the condos went in, the builders had to guarantee, without restrictions, that access to the canal's fishing and bulkhead would not be denied. You end up fishing in front of people's patio doors but as long as you are not a slob or make a lot of noise, there is no problem.

In season, April through June, the live-lining of herring or alewives—still legal in Jersey at this writing—is popular. Because of the stout currents in the canal, water column penetrators such as bucktails and shads are popular with locals.

CONTACT TIP: Reel Life Bait and Tackle, Point Pleasant, (732) 899-3506.

33
Brick Beach
Mantoloking, New Jersey

BEST MONTHS TO FISH: April to December (summers are slow).

RECOMMENDED METHODS: Bottom baits—clams and chunks and lures.

FISH YOU CAN EXPECT TO CATCH: Stripers, bluefish, occasional tunoids late summer.

HOW TO GET THERE: From exit 89 on the Garden State Parkway take Route 528 east to its end, then a right onto Route 135. The first two streets on the left in Mantoloking are popular. A mile south of there Route 135 splits. After that there is a gin mill, "Used to Be's," between the north- and south-bound lanes and across the street from a firehouse. A left after the fire barn will take you to the lot for Brick Beach. It's a piece of cake.

This is really two sections of the same beach—Brick Beach on the south and Montoloking on the north. Brick Beach has a good-sized parking lot for people who walk in. Buggies are allowed during the off season with a pass from Town Hall. Fishing for walk-in surfcasters is limited to the bathing after hours, say 9:00 P.M. to 6:00 A.M. during the summer. But, when the fishing is best, say September on, it is wide open for fisherman at both Montoloking and Brick.

There is nice structure interspersed with some bars that yield some decent stripers and, at times, bluefish until the Lord Himself won't have them. All the surfcasting standards among artificials are used here, especially if there are breaking fish. Live eels are effective. Although I know that rigged eels would work, people don't bother with them that much in this section of Jersey. Usual bottom baits are chunks or clams.

Use your head in the placement of bottom baits, selecting spots where a couple of sloughs intersect or where you can read a drop-off during the day. Wear Polaroids in daylight to penetrate the surface glare. If you find a nice hole for bait fishing, space your baits from the beach, not your rods down the beach. Where you put your rods is not as relevant as where you put the baits and seeing two rods that are close together makes them easier to watch and also to attend when a monster takes one down.

CONTACT TIP: Jersey Coast Bait and Tackle, Brick, (732) 451-1077.

Inlets served by jetties are more stable.

34
Manasquan Inlet
Brielle/Point Pleasant, New Jersey

BEST MONTHS TO FISH: April through December.

RECOMMENDED METHODS: Drifting live baits, plugging, and using eels with tin squids.

FISH YOU CAN EXPECT TO CATCH: Stripers, bluefish, and weakfish.

HOW TO GET THERE: From the south on the Garden State Parkway, take exit 88 and Route 88 (same numbers) to Point Pleasant, then head north on Route 35 until you can see the water on your left. Go right onto Broadway east. Where Broadway turns to the south you can take Ocean Avenue. There is a nice parking lot at the end of the inlet road. If you're coming from the north, leave the parkway at exit 98 for Route 35 south to Brielle. Take a right onto East Main then go east to a right onto Third Avenue.

The two jetties flanking Manasquan Inlet are fished with equal zeal and both enjoy public access and parking, provided that surfcasters go there at night. The only reason for that is customary day use of the beach fills the parking lot quickly. The big method here is to drift either live or dead spot or snapper blues. Naturally, if you have live ones and can keep them, you'll have an edge. Remember to watch for the early-fall mullet run, which is a sign that swimming plugs often do the trick. Come November, everything works.

We rate this inlet a little lower because it does not service as large a bay as some of the other inlets on the New Jersey shore. I can't emphasize enough that this is a place where you can walk upright to fish freely. You don't have to use face paint and crawl like a sniper. The best tide is the outgoing, but once it slackens regulars head for where the Point Pleasant Canal runs into the Manasquan River.

CONTACT TIP: Alex's Bait and Tackle, Point Pleasant Beach, (732) 295-9268, is right near the inlet.

35

Shark River Inlet
Belmar on the south, Avon on the north
New Jersey

BEST MONTHS TO FISH: May through December.

RECOMMENDED METHODS: Plugs and live-lining.

FISH THAT YOU CAN EXPECT TO CATCH: Stripers, blues, possible tunoids late summer.

HOW TO GET THERE: From the south use the Garden State Parkway then Route 138 east and follow the signs to Belmar. From the north leave the GSP and travel east to Bradley Beach then south on 40A. Any east or left turn will take you to Ocean Avenue in Avon-by-the-Sea; then head south until you hit the inlet.

We treat this inlet separately from the 20-mile stretch in Jetty Country (see spot 36) because all inlets have unique characteristics in their water flow that influence the fishing. For example, the Shark River does not serve as large a bay as many of the others, like that which serves Barnegat Bay. Here the opening between jetties is about 600 feet. Sanding in, which I have no measure of in this case, can reduce the tidal flow of this hot spot. So, while the tide moves well, it does not roar as much as some inlets elsewhere might. That is not to say that fishing is compromised, however. It seems to me that the length of distance from this outflow to the next in either direction would more than compensate for any reduced flow.

While this estuarine opening is flanked by jetties, both are fished with comparative zeal by the regulars whose distress will be heightened by seeing this spot in this book. Views from the air appear, I said appear, to give an edge to the south jetty on the Belmar side. Here the stones reach several hundred feet more to the east and there is even a bar on the south side where gamefish have to lurk. It's a no-brainer.

No doubt the water moves too well for bottom baits, especially if there are others fishing and there are bound to be. This is classic eel, spot, snapper, or mullet drifting water where you cast directly across and free spool seaward, as long as the others who are fishing are doing so in harmony. Otherwise, I would plug by casting long and allowing the lure to swing under tension off your rod tip. The best shot is to do this at night. If my granddaughter came home with a kid who fished Shark River in the daytime, I would find it hard to be nice.

CONTACT TIP: Brielle Bait and Tackle, Brielle, (732) 528-5720.

36
Manasquan to Long Branch
(Jetty Country)
New Jersey

BEST MONTHS TO FISH: April through December.

RECOMMENDED METHODS: Live baits, big swimmers, calico crabs, and tin squids.

FISH YOU CAN EXPECT TO CATCH: Stripers, bluefish, flounder, and weakfish—with tunoids in late summer.

HOW TO GET THERE: Go east on any of the parkway exits from Manasquan to Long Branch; they will lead to suitable shore roads—mostly Ocean Avenue—that are available the full length of this stretch.

Anyone from outside this North Jersey area would be overwhelmed by the thought of 121 jetties in a 20-mile stretch of shoreline. Of course, the count—done by the hangarounds of J&J Tackle, in Belmar, back when they commanded a greater following—included every string of stones, about one-third of which are not likely to produce a whole lot of striper fishing. Still, some of the eighty or so "good ones" are big and easy, luring stripers of all sizes. I must also take into account that some rock piles are more accessible than others, and parking varies from jetty to jetty. (Note that meters are policed all night in Belmar.) John Chiola once told me that occasionally someone comes along to challenge the right of anglers to fish certain jetties, but they always lose. Though it is part of the long shore from Manasquan to Long Branch, we have decided to treat the Shark River Inlet separately in order to both emphasize it and to address its nuances. Let's go fishing.

There is a good string of ten or more jetties in Spring Lake, but you can't get on all of them at the top of the tide. Consequently, regulars will wait for the water to lower before trying them. Because they cover with water, you can be sure the rocks will be slick. Area regulars have their favorites, which serve to fill the night with opportunity; they know which ones will be productive while they wait for others to be exposed by the tide. And, within each jetty, they know the lies that stripers like to use. It is a certainty that each place that has ever given up a fish is indelibly stored in their memory. Naturally, there is a certain competition among regulars to be the first to check a spot during a favored phase of tide. Exactly what tide phase is best for a particular location is usually a closely guarded secret, but often known by more than one angler. Be mindful of poorly shielded lights that might send stripers that are there hell west, and even the click of cleats upon the stones might be enough to spook a lineside. Thus, efforts to be the first on a rock pile, to reap the benefits of virgin territory, are no small part of the local cult. As I find myself saying more about the surfcasters than the surf fishing here, it is my hope that new anglers can draw a number of cogent lessons: first, that jetty fishing is a specific discipline under the greater god of surfcasting, and that it is, as a result, more dangerous, more demanding than those other shore fishing situations with which you may be confronted elsewhere; second, that most jetty anglers have paid their dues with a lifetime of sleepless nights or lost jobs or worse and have experienced the variety of social turmoil one might expect from spending one's nights at the shore instead of tending to normal business. Nothing shuts up a battered and bruised surfcaster more quickly than a newcomer who is asking a lot of questions and seeking a free ride on the coattails of that kind of dedication and history. This North Jersey territory is steeped in surfcasting tradition, and its jetties are no small part of it. Thus, anyone aspiring to become part of this exclusive corps would do well to prove his or her worth in the same hard way.

It improves from Manasquan north to a peak of opportunity around Deal and Asbury Park. Though they are revitalizing Asbury Park it is still dicey, not because of the fishing, but because of the big-city environment of homeless living under the boardwalk. The situation has you looking over your shoulder all the time. The Eighth Avenue "Flume," which runs with a will from Deal

Lake in Asbury Park every time it rains, doles out a steady diet of trapped herring (alewives) that were hatched out the previous spring. To mention this here is not to tell anything that locals haven't known since their first cast. Once you get to the north end of Long Branch, the jetties drop off in quality—eroded, low, and short.

Bait writes the book on methods. April alewife runs have sharpies using them alive, provided they can get and keep them. The potential for that doesn't end until late June. Come July, eels (both alive and rigged) come into play. A strong local flair for the use of rigged eels can be seen in the application of tin squids that are sewn into the eel's head. While lending enhanced castabililty, the squid gives the bait a better swim than God ever intended. During slow periods some like to use live calico crabs. As it is statewide, the September mullet run triggers a feeding binge that throws otherwise cagey and selective stripers off their guard. Metal (called "tin" farther north, regardless of true composition) comes into play, as do Rebels, Red Fins, Bombers, and Mambo Minnow swimmers. By fall (at these latitudes well into December) it is anything and anytime. Naturally, local surfcasters will accept some blues and weakfish as targets of opportunity, but, in this hard-core, highly esoteric subculture of surfmen, there is only one thing in life with meaning: a striped bass big enough to make a big man sweat.

CONTACT TIP: Jim's Bait and Tackle, Long Branch, (732) 229-9690.

Flat water and long wading provide great fly fishing at night.

37
Sandy Hook Point
Sandy Hook, New Jersey

BEST MONTHS TO FISH: April through December.

RECOMMENDED METHODS: Drifting baits or plugs and fly fishing.

FISH YOU CAN EXPECT TO CATCH: Stripers, bluefish, and weakfish. False albacore late summer some years.

HOW TO GET THERE: Take Route 36 east from the Garden State Parkway. At Highlands follow signs north for Sandy Hook. The end of the line is Fort Hancock. You can also follow the coastal road (Route 36) from Long Branch.

This northernmost location is a sandy spit dipping into the opening of Raritan Bay. The length of the Sandy Hook peninsula is 5 miles, which is no small reach into open water. One of the few openings not guarded by a jetty, the Hook is sandy shore that reaches well into the bay, forcing fishermen to wade considerable distances. With night fishing most often the drill here, it is wise to carry a compass in case of fog. Also, watch for passing vessels that will often throw enough of a wake to fill your waders. Have an abiding respect for currents; while they make the fishing what it is here, they pose some risk to the overzealous surfcaster. This is known as a scary spot for good reason.

The Hook dips below the surface 3 miles north of the last designated parking area at Fort Hancock. At the ranger station on the way in, officials issue free parking passes for night fishing and ticket you if you don't have one. As buggies are not allowed, this is a spot for surfmen young enough to hoof the 6-mile round trip with enough left in them for fishing. Even the guys who clap their hands between push-ups won't drag a suitable fish back over these distances. Usually they bring along a scale and camera in a backpack to prove that the expected really happened. And it often does. Bayside accessible, and not such a long walk for the public near Fort Hancock, is Plum Island, which is popular with wading fly fishermen. It is protected enough and shallow enough that you can use a floating line and skip the stripping basket.

Nobody can be certain, but one explanation for the Hook being what it is, particularly in late fall, is that it serves as host to returning Hudson River stripers—a population, of late, that has never seen better numbers. If Chesapeake and Delaware River fish happen by as well, it is doubly productive. This cowboy country is not quite worth the effort in summer, but certainly in spring and late fall it could be your best chance at a moose of a striper. Pack everything tight and light, use live eels and big plugs.

While the currents at the end are best, you can locate fish all along the way. The Bug Light at the tip of the Hook is a well-known and great spot. Outside of bathing seasons, the Sandy Hook shore adjacent to the parking lots is more popular because of accessibility.

CONTACT TIP: Giglio's Bait and Tackle, Sea Bright, (732) 741-0480.

38
Lighthouse Bay
South Amboy, New Jersey

BEST MONTHS TO FISH: Late April through June for stripers, blues and fluke in summer.

RECOMMENDED METHODS: Drifting baits and plugs.

FISH YOU CAN EXPECT TO CATCH: Stripers, bluefish, and fluke.

HOW TO GET THERE: Take the Garden State Parkway to exit 124, South Amboy and Route 9, then Bordentown Avenue east to the end and the parking lot.

Here is a spot that is influenced by the qualities of both Sandy Hook and the Raritan River. It makes the boys in North Jersey as well as those from Staten Island happy. Raritan Bay is known for good early-season striper fishing, as the bunker show up beforehand. Most anglers associate the Raritan with the south side, such as Keansburg and such, but some say this place is just as good if not better than the other side of the bay. My spies make the point that the fishing changes with the seasons. The best time to fish is late April through June for stripers. After that blues and fluke replace the stripers that have since migrated. Bait is the trick in spring, clam and bunker.

CONTACT TIP: Fred's Bait and Tackle, South Amboy, (732) 721-4747.

NEW YORK

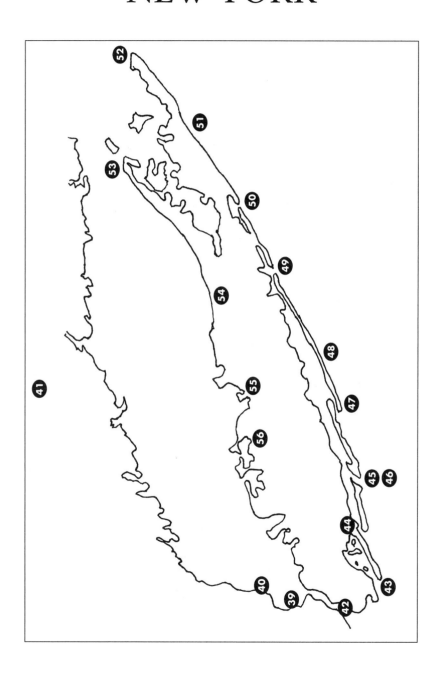

The Hudson River

The Hudson River Estuary stretches 153 miles from Troy to New York Harbor, nearly half the river's 315-mile course between Lake Tear of the Clouds, its source in the Adirondacks, and the Battery at the tip of Manhattan. This estuary feels the ocean's rising and falling tides along with shifting tidal currents all the way to Troy, New York. Salty seawater pushes up the estuary, diluted by freshwater runoff as it moves north. Eventually the estuary becomes fresh, even though it is still tidal. In years with average amounts of rainfall, spring runoff holds the leading edge of dilute seawater—the salt front—downriver between the Tappan Zee and Yonkers. As runoff slackens in summer, the salt front pushes northward to Newburgh Bay (river mile 55) and further to Poughkeepsie (river mile 75) in droughts. Rarely does brackish water extend north of Poughkeepsie. From Poughkeepsie to Troy it is still fresh water. More than 200 species of fish are found in the Hudson and its tributaries. The estuary's productivity is ecologically and economically valuable to much of the Atlantic Coast. The Hudson ranks second only to Chesapeake Bay in East Coast striper production. (Though that important role could be trumped by continued Delaware River enhanced production.) Tidal marshes, mudflats, and other significant habitats in and along the estuary support a great diversity of life, including endangered species like the shortnose sturgeon.

As with so many rivers in industrialized parts of America, pollution, in this case polychlorinated biphenyl contamination, has left its mark upon both the river and its fishes. The EPA estimates that between ¼ million and 1.3 million pounds of PCBs were discharged into the Hudson from two General Electric capacitor manufacturing plants located in Hudson Falls and Fort Edward. Striped bass have been found with such high levels of PCBs in their flesh that they qualified as hazardous waste. It has never been determined if this substance is a carcinogen but it is highly suspect, and that suspicion has acted as a protection for striped bass—taking the price off their head—when these fish were judged unsuitable for the marketplace.

After over 30 years of environmental initiatives to reverse generations of pollution and neglect, the Hudson River Estuary, with its rich history and abundant natural resources, is again attracting sportsmen and women to its shores.

The Public Trust Doctrine states that the waters, the rivers, the fish that swim in these rivers belong to the people of this nation. No one has the right to deny this access to the people and developers must provide access. (Courtesy, in part: New York DEP and the Hudson River Fisherman's Association.)

Regulations at this writing—and we say it that way because they can change—are that no fishing license is required below Troy Dam and the striper season has been March 16 to November 30.

39

Piermont Pier
Piermont, New York

BEST MONTHS TO FISH: Mid-March to June. Late April is big.

RECOMMENDED METHODS: Bottom baits—blood worms and alewife or shad chunks.

FISH YOU CAN EXPECT TO CATCH: Stripers, often quite large.

HOW TO GET THERE: Take Piermont Road (State Highway 340) to the center of town to Piermont Avenue then to Ferry Road and follow signs. Park at the beginning of the pier near the Little League field where there is ample parking.

This west bank pier extends a mile into the river, and there are plenty of areas to park and fish along it. People deal with the distance by getting a yearly parking pass to drive on the pier, which, for out-of-sate visitors, is climbing in cost every year. Many Hudson River Fishermen's Association members use bicycles with baskets and rod holders—similar to those in use on the Cape Cod Canal—to make the journey out to the end of the pier. This spot vies as one of the most popular Hudson River spring fishing spots. As with the rest of the river locations, fishing is mainly done with bottom worms and chunks with some occasional lure use. The springtime striper run draws a lot of crowds. Anglers to whom I spoke said they preferred the north side of the pier, when they can get a spot. Blood worms, when you can acquire them, seem to have an edge. The pier is open from 6 A.M. to 9 P.M. all year and is a favorite spot year-round but particularly good during the spring spawning run. Many prefer the end area to fish. While fishing is about equal to other Hudson River locations, we lowered the rating one unit because of the length of the pier and restrictions on night fishing.

CONTACT TIP: Davis Sports Shop, Sloatsburg, (845) 753-2198.

40
Croton Bay
Croton Point Park
Croton-on-Hudson, New York

BEST MONTHS TO FISH: Mid-March to June. Late April is big.

RECOMMENDED METHODS: Bottom baits—worms and chunks, some lures.

FISH YOU CAN EXPECT TO CATCH: Stripers.

HOW TO GET THERE: From the south, take the New York State Thruway (north) to exit 9 (Tarrytown). Proceed north on Route 9 for approximately 10 miles and exit at Croton Point Avenue. Turn left at the end of ramp then left at light. The park entrance is straight ahead. From the east, use the Merritt Parkway (south) or New England Thruway (south) to 1-287 west to the New York State Thruway north to exit 9 (Tarrytown). Proceed north on Route 9 for approximately 10 miles and exit at Croton Point Avenue. Turn left at the end of ramp then left at light. The park entrance is straight ahead.

The nearby Croton River has dumped sediment into the bay over the years, thus creating a shallow flat that extends out into the river on the Hudson's east bank. When the sun warms the shallows, the bass move out of the channel and onto the flat in serious numbers on their way both to and from the spawning grounds. It is one of those natural draws for which striper hounds are always looking. A joy in this spot is that a Westchester County park serves the very place where the fishing is allaying any access issues in the bay itself. Bass do run partway up the Croton River, but access there is tricky and unless you are a commando type it is probably not a good idea to crowd the river. The train bridge on your left at the park entrance looks very promising, but you would have to use your head over its use.

Most of the spring fishing here is bottom fishing with blood worms. Herring or alewife chunks are popular during this season of alewife runs as well. They also chunk American white shad if bait acquisition becomes an issue. While efforts are predominantly bait, a lot of sharpies still use plugs and other artificials. It would seem to me to be a perfect place to fly fish, but I couldn't find anyone who said they had seen it done. Kayaks and canoes are popular here. You may need the Westchester County pass, but I'm told that fishing is over by the time that they require it.

CONTACT TIP: Wades Bait and Tackle, Hawthorne, (914) 948-7364.

41
Troy Dam
Hudson River
Troy, New York

BEST MONTHS TO FISH: Mid-April through early July.

RECOMMENDED METHODS: Alewives or shad chunks, blood worms, big jigs, swimming and surface plugs.

FISH YOU CAN EXPECT TO CATCH: Stripers, white shad, and largemouth as well as smallmouth bass.

HOW TO GET THERE: From I–90 in downtown Albany, take Route 787 north for just under 6 miles to a traffic light. Take a right turn to Green Island on Tibbits Avenue. A couple of blocks on the left there is an old Ford plant parking lot where anglers park, then walk down the bank.

Current, well-aerated powerhouse outflow, and both ground and live alewives to chum fish in, are the key ingredients to this first Hudson River barrier. Few stripers make it over the dam and even then they require a spring tide and perfect high water conditions. Anglers gather at this west bank location every spring to cash in on this curious set of both natural and man-made conditions. Fish with 20- or even 30-pound-test lines to deal with the combination of crowds, current, and sometimes big fish to forty pounds.

Regulars watch for a 50-degree water temperature that occurs in late April while coinciding with the alewife run. Then fishers line the shore and toss live or freshly dead alewives upcurrent, letting the bait drift naturally in the white water under the powerhouse. Another favorite choice is to cast big swimmers, which simulate local baits. There is a very special top-water action with surface plugs in June. Also, drift deep with oversized jigs with twister tails as an effective way to efficiently probe the depths in this current.

The most popular tides are on the moons, but avoid fishing during low water because the shallows make stripers spooky. Though fish can be taken around the clock, the best time is dark early morning; this is both a universal witching hour and a means of avoiding the mob. While fishers can score all summer and fall, those times are a mere shadow of spring's whoppertunities.

There is everything here including sturgeon, smallmouth, pike, carp, perch, and shad, which of late have been improving their run. Fish these with 6-pound mono tied directly to a dead-drifted shad dart.

CONTACT TIP: River Basin Sport Shop, Catskill, (518) 943-2111.

42
Manhattan Fishing Accesses
New York

BEST MONTHS TO FISH: Mid-April through December.

RECOMMENDED METHODS: Bottom baits of alewife, menhaden or shad chunks, big jigs, swimming and surface plugs.

FISH YOU CAN EXPECT TO CATCH: Stripers and bluefish

HOW TO GET THERE: Most of this collection of spots is on the east bank of the Hudson River in both Upper and Lower Manhattan, so an intimacy with the city is necessary to take full advantage of the public property involved. It would be impossible to relate specific directions to all 31 of the locations listed here.

Probably the best of the fishing in these spots should be done during the day because of risky city environmental concerns. That said, for those who are not concerned with security issues, many of these docks are lighted after dark, and light creates shadows that appeal to stripers lurking on the dark side of a shadow in order to jump passing baitfish. This is the same kind of specialized fishing that is applied in bridge fishing. Stripers, and especially the big ones, will appear as dark-on-gray fish silhouettes either waiting or swimming along the shadow edge. Places where currents form up just right, and on the Hudson there is plenty of that, will hold fish on a regular basis. Bucktail jigs in the larger, say 8/0 size, delivered with the heaviest gear are the ticket. I have fished this way elsewhere and have spent much time on the Cape comparing notes with New York City regulars who also utilized this method. As to just which spots provide this sort of opportunity, it is a matter of individual preference. Staten Island offers three fishing piers—Lemon Creek, St. George's, and Ocean. Other than those three, here is the list of either city- or state-owned piers, docks, and bulkheads in Manhattan for your perusal. Except for those marked with an asterisk (*) all are handicapped accessible.

LOWER MANHATTAN
West 27th Street, West 27th and West Side Highway
Hudson River Park, from 59th and West Side Highway to Battery Place—lighting and bathrooms
Pier 54, West 13th and West Side Highway
Pier 40, West Houston and West Street—lighting, covered and bathrooms
South Side of Pier 34, Canal and West Street—lighting
Pier 25 and 26, Moore Street and West Street—lighting and bathrooms
Rockefeller Park, Battery Park City—lighting and bathrooms
Esplanade, Battery Park City—lighting and bathrooms
Historic Battery Park, Battery Park City—lighting and bathrooms
Dover Street Pier, South Street and Dover Street—lighting
Southeast Access, from South Street Seaport to north of Rutgers Street—lighting
East River Park, Jackson Street to 13th Street along FDR Drive—lighting and bathrooms
Stuyvesant Cove, East 18th Street to 25th Street—lighting
East River Esplanade, 36th Street to 38th Street

UPPER MANHATTAN

Roosevelt Island, West Road—lighting

Light House Park, north tip of Roosevelt Island—lighting

Wards Island Park, Wards Island—bathrooms*

107th Street Pier, 107th Street—covered

FDR Access, 42nd Street to Triborough Bridge

Randalls Island Park, Randalls Island—lighting*

Harlem River Greenway, 125th to 145th Street

215th and 9th Avenue, 215th to 216th off 9th Avenue*

Inwood Hill Park, long walk to good access*

Dyckman Street Pier, Dyckman Street off Riverside Drive

Dyckman Boat Marina, Dyckman Street off Riverside Drive—bathrooms

Fort Washington Park, from Dyckman Street to 145th Street—bathrooms*

Riverbank State Park, access via 145th Street off Riverside Drive—bathrooms*

Marginal Street, end of West 125th and Marginal Street

Riverside Park, 79th–129th Streets along Henry Hudson Parkway—bathrooms

79th Street Boat Basin, West 79th Street off Riverside Drive—covered

68th–69th Street Pier, access on the west end of 69th Street—lighting and covered

* = Not handicapped accessible

CONTACT TIP: Jack's Bait and Tackle, Bronx, (718) 885-2042.

NEW YORK/LONG ISLAND

No doubt the greatest concentration of rabid surfcasters on the planet is in New York City. Their presence in an urban environment of that size indicates that opportunities for practice of their craft have got to be pretty good. Along with all the traditional locations enumerated here, New Yorkers enjoy an astounding level of opportunity for shore fishing right in the city itself. Indeed, in the deep of night, great numbers and sizes of linesides are lured into the shadows of well-lighted docks, where sharpies who know how to find them succeed with impunity. The many bridges that lace the city offer similar, if not equal, opportunities, though admittedly now clouded by terrorism concerns. The practice of what I call "Commando Fishing" where silence, discretion, and streetwise inner-city practice are no small part of fishing, is alive and well everywhere that stripers are fished in this state. I raise my glass to those who dare risk a mugging, a towing, or territorial disputes in the name of striper fishing, and although I need not follow in their footsteps at my age, I know all too well what it entails.

In my tour of Cape Cod surfcasting that began over forty years ago, I had the pleasure of befriending any number of New Yorkers with whom I shared many mid-watch hunts for striped bass. I found these surfmen to be aggressive because of where they came from; I found them hardworking because of an ethic that had been instilled in them; and, lastly, I found them dedicated because of an all-abiding love for both the high surf and the greatest gamefish of our time.

Sad to say, Long Island is cursed with both over-development and a population that demands privacy. It asserts its territorial

(Courtesy Charlie Taylor)

rights well beyond the borders of its own property—an injustice not at all uncommon elsewhere on the Striper Coast. Therefore, in keeping with my mission here, I have not sought to disclose spots that are not reasonably accessible to outsiders.

43
Breezy Point
Rockaway, New York, New York

BEST MONTHS TO FISH: May to Mid-December. Summers are sometimes slow.

RECOMMENDED METHODS: Swimming plugs, rigged and live eels.

FISH YOU CAN EXPECT TO CATCH: Stripers, bluefish, and weakfish.

HOW TO GET THERE: Take the Belt Parkway east to Flatbush Avenue, then head south over Marine Parkway Bridge. Coming off the bridge, take the first left and follow signs to Fort Tilden for a National Park Service parking permit.

The Breezy Point jetty is one of the more reliable and accessible spots in the New York City area. Moreover, my contacts reluctantly claim it as one of the more underrated, underfished spots on the Striper Coast. Be aware, however, that the jetty is a dangerous place because of the slick stones. It gets "real snotty" with strong winds out of any of the southern quadrants, blowing pushy water over the top. For that reason, wear Korkers or cleats to improve your footing, because even rescue doesn't like going out there. Nonetheless, slick rocks are a price that regulars are more than

The jetty is good, but you can also fish the open beach.

willing to pay for a steady dole of moby linesides available there, particularly during the fall months.

The tip of the jetty is best, because it provides access to the strong currents that develop there on either tide. A favored method is to fish big swimming plugs in the deep of night, but avoid teasers or droppers, as the current presses them against leaders, rendering them less effective. Old-time traditional New

York swimmers like Dannys, Atoms—the big stuff—are what works here. Bucktails with pork rind are also popular. Unique to this prominent Rockaway opening is that the current most often flows seaward, regardless of tide, because rising water back-eddies. Thus, it is possible to feed a plug into the current to gain added distance in fishing coverage. Winds that support the natural movement of the water are most popular: southeast on the incoming at the tip of the jetty. During northeast and northwest winds, the west sides of the jetty produce all through the incoming.

After the bathing season ends in September, a buggy can be a great help here. Four-wheelers with the appropriate permit (available at the Fort Tilden office) from Gateway National Recreational Area can be used to run the beach out to the Breezy Point jetty at the west end.

Increasing numbers of surfcasters are recognizing that the beach area between the Park Service office, on both sides of the peninsula, as well as the jetty, are highly productive in the fall, and the later the better. Not all surfcasters care for mountain goating their way over slick rock piles. Expect good daytime action in the fall, and you can beach drive around six miles into Jacob Riis Park to the east.

As part of the Gateway National Recreation Area, the Park Service at the Fort Tilden Headquarters, (718) 318-4300, issues two kinds of permits for fishing: the fishing permit, which allows you to park during night hours and for which you must have fishing equipment; and, 4-wheel-drive permit that can be used for a buggy in the off season from September 1 to December 31 and the early spring. The cost of either permit at this writing, and you know how that goes, is $50. You do not need both.

CONTACT TIP: Woodcleft Fishing Station, Freeport, (516) 378-8748. There are also fishing reports by dialing (516) 977-2088.

44
Silver Point/Long Beach
Silver Point County Park
Long Island
Lawrence, New York

BEST MONTHS TO FISH: May to Mid-December. Summers are sometimes slow.

RECOMMENDED METHODS: Swimming plugs, bucktail jigs, live eels, clam baits on the bottom.

FISH YOU CAN EXPECT TO CATCH: Stripers, bluefish, and weakfish.

HOW TO GET THERE: From the Southern Parkway, Route 27, take Rockaway Boulevard south to Cedarhurst or Lawrence. Go straight until you go over a bridge then right onto Atlantic Boulevard and follow the signs to Atlantic Beach. In sight of the water, go right to a one-horse town called Lookout. You'll see the jetty on the right or west.

The Silver Point jetty, which is about 100 yards long, is a little busted up but it still commands a good access to the currents formed by both the rise and fall of waters from the East Rockaway Inlet. Dropping tides, as with all inlets, have the edge. The back marsh is loaded with forage, producing baits that will appeal to passing gamefish. Stripers will go in the back, so the quiet marsh fishing is a great place to wade and listen for the feeding sounds of whatever gamefish need to swill on—grass shrimp, small crabs, juvie sea worms, or eels.

This spot gets less attention because of the opportunity in nearby Breezy Point and Jones Inlet that flank it only a few miles on either side. Still, if the other spots are hot, why wouldn't Silver Point hold fish as well?

The front beach is wildly popular in the fall when the migration is on. The out-of-the-way nature of this spot makes it an easy place to park and fish. The parking lot parking permit—no ORV use—is $20. If your situation is appealing, say visiting family or on business, I would pay for the parking pass and walk out to the jetty to fish.

CONTACT TIP: Comb's Bait and Tackle, Amityville, (631) 264-3525.

45
Point Lookout
Jones Inlet (West)
Long Beach
Point Lookout, Long Island, New York

BEST MONTHS TO FISH: May to Mid-December. Summers are sometimes slow.

RECOMMENDED METHODS: Swimming plugs, bucktail jigs, rigged and live eels, and bottom baits.

FISH YOU CAN EXPECT TO CATCH: Stripers, bluefish, and weakfish.

HOW TO GET THERE: Leave the Long Island Expressway, Route 495, at Roslyn south, onto the Merrick Road. About five miles after Merrick, take a right onto Loop Parkway (signs for Lido Beach and Point Lookout) and it will drop you into Point Lookout.

The entire east end of Long Beach Island is covered with jetty stones. There is similarity in the opportunity and tight control of the area that we find on all of Long Island's non-federal parks. Again, you have the currents spawned by the back pond, both Middle and East Bays, that cause a good movement of water. There is a short jetty out front and some good protected back fishing. I'm told that weakfish opportunity is better on this west side of Jones Inlet, but you can only take advantage of that during years when the weakfish are up on their cycle. Stripers are more likely, but we all fish for whatever we can get anyway. You can park on the street back a ways from the jetty stones.

CONTACT TIP: Scotty's Fishing Station, Point Lookout, (516) 432-4665.

46
Jones Inlet (West End 2)
Jones Beach State Park
Wantagh, New York

BEST MONTHS TO FISH: May to December (mid-summer is slow).

RECOMMENDED METHODS: Swimming plugs, live baits live lined—snapper, bunker, or eels.

FISH YOU CAN EXPECT TO CATCH: Stripers, bluefish, and weakfish.

HOW TO GET THERE: Going east from the Long Island Expressway take Glen Cove south after Roslyn Heights until it changes to Meadowbrook Parkway and follow it to the end right onto Bay Parkway west. There are signs for the West End 2 parking lot. The inlet is to the west.

This is the other side of the inlet from Point Lookout, but public access and a better command of the inlet currents give it a higher rating. While it is something of a walk out to the Jones Inlet jetty, it provides a flatter, easier set of stones to walk on and is, in effect, a fishing platform reaching about 150 yards into the sea. The most popular time to fish is the last three hours of the outgoing tide at night. Fish the current on your right or west for the best fishing. Even so, watch the east side of the breakwater in that pocket alongside the jetty. While plugs are popular, bait fishing produces as well. There is some bait fishing along the Jones Beach sand in summer, but look for big fish early October to late November.

In order to park here, a night fishing pass is required, with the only legal purpose being to fish. I would avoid fishing the beach during the day in bathing season. Lifeguards would probably stop you anyway.

CONTACT TIP: Causeway Bait and Tackle, Wantagh, (516) 785-3223.

47

Captree State Park
Babylon/Fire Island, New York

BEST MONTHS TO FISH: May through October.

RECOMMENDED METHODS: Bottom baits during the day, light spinning and fly fishing nights.

FISH YOU CAN EXPECT TO CATCH: Stripers, bluefish, blackfish, flounder, porgy, sea bass, mixed bag.

HOW TO GET THERE: From any major east/west highway, take the Robert Moses Causeway south that will lead to the park about five miles south of West Islip.

Both avid fishermen and novice anglers enjoy the excellent fishing opportunities at Captree. The area is known for its sea bass, summer flounder, or fluke that arrive in mid-summer. Blackfish perk up in spring and fall. Striper fishing goes on in the deep night in the back among the barrier islands during reduced boat traffic. Currents are great, and this is an ideal place for sharpies with light tackle—fly or spinning—wading, as there is water on three sides of the area's natural salt marshes in the back. In Captree's front, currents are fierce from Great South Bay and I would give that south side of the island the edge because of it. Nevertheless, don't even think of fishing from the causeway bridge. They'll skin you alive!

This is not rough-and-tumble surfcasting like they do at Montauk. Rather, it is more sedate for old-timers day fishing or to bring their grandchildren. Visitors can fish from piers, which include two handicapped-accessible piers. You can find all this when you arrive if you bear right to the picnic area where there are restrooms and snacks. Parking is (or at least was when this was written) $6.

CONTACT TIP: Augie's Custom Tackle, Babylon, (631) 669-9837.

48
Fire Island
Fire Island National Seashore
Patchogue, New York

BEST MONTHS TO FISH: May to December, but October and November are best.

RECOMMENDED METHODS: Swimming plugs and all customary artificials of the striper surf.

FISH YOU CAN EXPECT TO CATCH: Stripers, bluefish, and weakfish.

HOW TO GET THERE: From New York City, on any major east/west highway, such as the Long Island Expressway, take the Robert Moses Causeway south that will lead to Fire Island about five miles south of West Islip. Further east you can take the William Floyd Parkway south to Fire Island.

The Fire Island Inlet is not as popular as those nearer to the city. The inlet itself is no longer guarded by a jetty on the south side

There is a lot of open beach fishing in the fall.

and is sand. Short of the inlet, there is a rinky-dink little jetty of no real importance but I would still try it.

The best aspect of this area is the drivable 8 miles to which the buggy-equipped surf fisher gains access for the fall migration. Two jurisdictions are involved here—Robert Moses State Park and Gateway National Seashore—and both require beach permits. The Gateway permit is free, but rules regarding beach use vary too much from year to year to justify enumeration here. However, the same common sense and regulation issues used elsewhere would apply. And, while there is a fee for Moses, the permit can be used in other state areas, like the one at Montauk. The Fire Island (FINS) ORV/beach-buggy permit was $50 in 2007. Remember, if you drive out to Fire Island Inlet's south side with a buggy, park above the high-water mark, as there have been a number of vehicles flooded here. Driving the waterline in the fall, when stripers and blues are migrating, is a favored way to spot schools of fish. At night, regulars will stop periodically to test the water with a plug.

While the best of Fire Island is the inlet, which is approached from the southeast side, don't overlook the beach on the north side, which your south-side over-sand vehicle permit entitles you to access in the fall. There is good current on this north side as well and current means gamefish. The north bank of Fire Island Inlet is looking across at Jones Beach. (The inlet is really a Jones Beach breakthrough.) Most of the water traded in Great South Bay is coming through Fire Island Inlet so it is watched closely by area mechanized surfcasters.

CONTACT TIP: Captree Bait and Tackle, Babylon, (631) 321-1499.

49
Moriches Inlet
Fire Island National Seashore
Center Moriches, Long Island, New York

BEST MONTHS TO FISH: May to early December, but October and November are best.

RECOMMENDED METHODS: Swimming plugs, chunks, and fly fishing.
FISH YOU CAN EXPECT TO CATCH: Stripers, bluefish, and weakfish.
HOW TO GET THERE: Either from Route 495 or the Sunrise Expressway (Route 27), take the Shirley exit and follow William Floyd Parkway south.

There is similarity between all the South Shore inlets in that the currents and jetties that guard them are the main draw and are the reason for inclusion here. Like the other jetty-flanked inlets, you have to be part mountain goat. For Moriches, undercover agents tell me the most popular tide is the last two hours up and the first two down. In mainland terms that translates to the worst tide because the closer you get to Montauk, the more disinformation is circulated and you are getting close to Montauk. If it were up to me I would fish the last two hours out to dead low slack. There is less water and the fish are more confined as well as changing position. Many diehards, however, will fish the drop all the way down. The main article in the inlet itself is swimming plugs at night, but just about everything is used during the good fall fishing found here. During summer, people will bait fish along the edges of the current with chunks. It is also possible to walk the back pond from the inlet to listen for feeding linesides in the deep of night. That small island in the back looks promising. Such protected backwaters are perfect for fly fishing.

The safest and shortest approach is from the east, where it is possible to reach the inlet on foot. If you want to approach the inlet from the west, which is a 6½-mile trip over-sand, your FINS beach permit is good as this is all Fire Island. Washouts are common and change the hazards of driving all the time; thus, from year to year it's hard to predict what you are going to run into in your efforts to approach from the west. As with most of Long Island's South Shore, full beach driving privileges begin September 15, but the serious migratory activity of gamesters coming down the beach will not begin until late October, when it builds with each passing day.

CONTACT TIP: J&J Sports, Patchogue, (631) 654-2311.

50
Shinnecock Inlet
Hampton Bays, Long Island, New York

BEST MONTHS TO FISH: May to early December, but October and November are best.

RECOMMENDED METHODS: Plugs and live eels.

FISH YOU CAN EXPECT TO CATCH: Stripers and bluefish.

HOW TO GET THERE: Take the Hampton Bays exit off Route 27 for the west side; cross the Ponquogue Bridge to the dune road and go left to the old Coast Guard Station. The east side is approached by over-sand vehicle from Southampton. The beach run is about four miles to the inlet (county beach permit required).

The west jetty that guards this fast-water inlet is the easier of the two approaches and is popular during southeast and northwest winds. No off-road vehicle is necessary. The east-side hot spot— where you need a buggy and which accommodates self-contained

Shinnecock is cow country.

vehicles—is a place at the jetty's end called the "Jungle." The word around here is that northwest winds move the current closer and that east winds help the casting: it is another one of those debates that rage about fishing and its more popular places. Common to both sides is the value of dropping water, particularly in the fall, but that is not to say that there is not some good fishing in the off-season and during the rising tide. Indeed, there is a lot to be said for avoiding crowds around here, even at the expense of missing the season's peak.

The off-road over-sand vehicle pass used on the east side is for residents only, so I wouldn't even think of fishing on that side as it is a four-mile walk to the inlet. Even then, your car would probably be gone when you got back. Once you are this far east, there is a growing influence generated by the currents of Montauk.

CONTACT TIP: Oakland's, Hampton Bays, (631) 728-5900.

51
Nepeague Beach
Montauk, New York

BEST MONTHS TO FISH: September through November.

RECOMMENDED METHODS: Plugs and lures.

FISH YOU CAN EXPECT TO CATCH: Stripers, bluefish, and weakfish; occasional tunoids early fall.

HOW TO GET THERE: Go west along the beach from Montauk or watch for beach access turns along Route 27 after Heather Hills. (Over-sand vehicle recommended.)

Nepeague Beach lies west of Montauk, running from Heather Hills to the Montauk town line, a distance of almost 5 miles. Although this rocky stretch suffers a great deal of erosion, sometimes causing buggy drivers to leave the shore to circumvent impassable areas, it does offer a chance to cover a stretch of shoreline adjacent to Montauk during the migration season. One of the rare open beach hot spots in this book, there is a lot of room to fish and it is a chance to escape the mobs just east of here.

According to locals, lures are by far the most popular method in this run-and-gun setting. Because it is a shallow area, the best fishing is on the incoming tide; north winds, from the back, are most popular because they add distance to the cast. Driving is prohibited between 10:00 A.M. and 6:00 P.M. during the summer, but after September 15 this beach is open around the clock (with proper permit, available from the East Hampton Town Hall). The $200 non-resident fee has to be a misprint. This spot is kid sister to Montauk Point.

CONTACT TIP: Freddie's Tackle Shop, Montauk, (631) 668-5520.

52
Montauk Point (Long Island)
Montauk, New York

BEST MONTHS TO FISH: May through early December, but fall is best.

RECOMMENDED METHODS: Plugs and lures.

FISH YOU CAN EXPECT TO CATCH: Stripers, bluefish, weakfish and occasional tunoids.

HOW TO GET THERE: Go east on Route 27 to land's end in Montauk. (Over-sand vehicle is optional.)

(Courtesy Walter Hingley)

Anytime you take on the job of writing about a place like Montauk, the problem becomes one of perspective. The surf fishing at Montauk could be a book in itself. Just limiting yourself to the hot spots within the hot spot becomes a challenge. Thus, in the name of brevity, I will limit myself to those observations that will be of the most service in the face of all the born-in-New-York cloak and dagger secrecy that drips from Long Island.

Montauk Point is a place where the currents of a hundred sources converge. Depending on wind and tide, the water can be moving in any given direction, gathering and sweeping bait as it goes. In addition to being an usually productive place to fish, it is eminently well known. Consequently, Montauk's curse is that it is the prime fishing spot for New York City surfcasters—no small following—who are all after the glamour species on public

One of the top surfcasting locations, Montauk can be memorable.
(Courtesy Walter Hingley)

property. Moreover, it is highly accessible to the foot traveler, which only contributes to the crowding.

Generally speaking, the north side—North Bar and False Bar—is favored during north winds. East winds, if they are light enough, tend to move currents and bait in, which improves the fishing, but once an east wind picks up to around 15 knots, water can become weedy and silty, making things impossible—a common intensity-dependent situation. Worth mentioning is the fact that a heavy rain will cause clay along the shore to discolor the water enough to shut fishing down. Tide preferences vary with the many locations spread around the curve and even then are reliant upon wind.

Montauk is like no other hot spot on the Striper Coast.

Thankfully, Montauk is like no other hot spot on the Striper Coast. As long as there is even the most remote chance of a run of fish, there will be large collections of anglers under the light from all over the Northeast. Even during the so-called low end times, say weeknights at 2:00 A.M., it is often necessary to forage for a spot from which to cast. In some ways the place is justifiably famous but in others the fame is related more to the consequences of too many surfcasters in too small an area, in spite of it being one of the biggest places where surfcasting is carried out. If the fishing is good the numbers will be outrageous. Cell phones bristle with every throwback. Moreover, if the stripers are collected in a specific location within the location, the numbers of anglers will concentrate. This leads to a lot of intense jockeying for favorable fishing positions with no small amount of acrimonious interaction the result. You can be fishing knee deep in your waders trying to avoid hitting a wet-suiter with your plug while someone in sneakers or pattern leather shoes casts over your head. Commonly, a surfman beaches a fish hauling it up high enough so as to prevent its loss. Once the fish is secured, the fisher turns to resume his position on the surfline only to find three others, having seen his success, now fishing where he had been. Need I finish this story?

Long Island's East End is also famous for "skishing," which is a wet suit rendition of shore fishing that permits the angler to utilize the buoyancy of the wet suit to swim a little further from shore in order to gain access to any number of offshore rocks that serve as a suitable fishing platform. This is particularly popular on False Bar and North Bar. A highly controversial manifestation of extreme surfcasting often labeled as a nutbag choice for the 6-knot rip currents that swing through Montauk's surf, skishing is also used to troll the rips out front.

Many knowing Montauk regulars also see it as just one more way to compete for a place to fish at a place where spots run out early. I am convinced that skishing, while productive angling-wise for those willing to take it on, is just one more means of dealing with competition, even if it does sometimes mean being

Big stripers prowl both sand and stone here.

picked up by a charter boat. Perhaps this behavior reflects an entire subculture that was raised to compete. If surfcasting lost its innocence, then it happened at Montauk and to some degree skishing had a hand in it. Still, Montauk's reputation for surf fishing is without dispute.

The shadow of Montauk Light is a natural gathering place for gamefish, and surfcasting attention is devoted to the easiest spots to get to (trout fishermen know this) or those with a run of fish in progress. A good bunch of stripers or bluefish is discovered quickly and the consequential results are evident to everyone.

However, solitude is sometimes available off to the sides at the more difficult places to reach that are down the beach below the private property up high and inland. The tougher the going among the melon-sized boulders strewn along the shore, the less likely that other surfcasters are to be working the foam. Miles of rocky shore entertain the multitudes here and there is a lot of room for innovation.

On foot, there are as many proponents of the south side of the light. It is a case of how far a surfcaster is willing to walk.

Forty-pound linesides are common.

Don't overlook both Rocky and Culloden Points on the north side, a few miles short of Montauk Light. One informant told me that many is the occasion—before cell phones—that the real job was being done there while others were skunking out at Montauk proper. Here but not there has always been part of the surfman's repertoire.

Naturally, an over-sand vehicle extends one's angling radius, enhancing the opportunity to avoid crowds. Three jurisdictions are involved in issuing beach permits: the state handles the lighthouse area; Suffolk County handles Shagwong; and Ditch Planes issues town permits. The requirements (four-wheel drive and the usual jack, shovel, board, tire gauge, and tow rope) are the same for all three.

Just as you are apt to see anybody and everybody fishing, you'll find all methods in use, from drifting live pogies carried by elaborate bait wells to chunks of frozen ones. From bucktails to poppers, if it has ever worked for stripers and blues, you'll see it at Montauk. Some generalizations that work everywhere: poppers and tin by day; swimmers by night. Whatever Montauk is—and it is a mecca for fanatical surfcasters—it is a multiple of itself in the fall. Just how early the insanity begins, or how late in December it ends, is the wild card. Never take a top-rated hot spot lightly as this is one of the best locations on the Striper Coast. Just be careful.

CONTACT TIP: Altenkirch Bait and Tackle, Hampton Bays, (631) 728-4110.

53

Orient Point
Greenport, New York

BEST MONTHS TO FISH: May through December, but fall is best.

RECOMMENDED METHODS: Plugs and lures for bass and blues; worms and crabs for blackfish (tog).

FISH YOU CAN EXPECT TO CATCH: Stripers, bluefish, and tog.

HOW TO GET THERE: Go east on Route 48 or 25 out of Riverhead and Route 48 out of Greenport. Follow the signs.

The tip of this Long Island north-fork peninsula offers shore fishing opportunities similar to those at Montauk. It is a bit rockier and more protected but less crowded. Thanks to a surprisingly large area of state land and county parks, access is among the best on Long Island. From Horton Point, on the west, all the way around the tip of Orient to the ferry slip is a good 13 miles. While you can't fish it all, there are ten or twelve pull-offs along the road where you can go down to the water and fish ¼ mile or more on either side. Truman Beach is a popular spot, as is the shore between the gut and the ferry landing (the southeast corner), but the opportunities can vary with time, tide, and wind to create potential for them all. Onshore north and nor'west winds are okay so long as they are not two-flaggers.

Oddly enough, the spot that ought to be hot, Plum Gut, has little to offer the surfcaster. From the Orient Point/New London ferry you can see the finger of stones reaching seaward on the west side of the channel. This may be one of the most dangerous spots in this book, as I am told that surfcasters are commonly washed off these stones, which reach out a long way into the currents of Gardiners Bay. Because I have no use for extreme surfcasting, if I were you, I wouldn't go there. It seems that the really working water is out of reach, making this more of a boat fishing hot spot.

Keep Orient Point in mind if a severe east storm or southern quadrant winds huff up and spoil the rest of Long Island. There is protection here and options that can keep you fishing when others are playing canasta behind shuttered windows elsewhere.

Plug fishing holds the greatest fascination here but, once summer bluefishing starts, there is interest in chunking the bottom. Of course, like everywhere worth listing, the target species is stripers, but keep in mind that Orient Point may be the best blackfish (tautog) place on the entire island, with two great runs at each end of the season—May and October—and it ain't exactly shabby in between. Use sea worms in spring and little green crabs in fall. Split the big ones with your knife before baiting up. The season lingers here, according to my spies, right up until Christmas. Tautog are awesome eating and last forever when vac-sealed and frozen.

CONTACT TIP: A. P. White, Greenport, (631) 477-0008.

54
Long Island North Shore
New York

BEST MONTHS TO FISH: April through November.

RECOMMENDED METHODS: Plugs and lures for bass and blues; worms and crabs for tog.

FISH YOU CAN EXPECT TO CATCH: Stripers, tautog, and bluefish.

HOW TO GET THERE: Because this is a collection of spots, areas are all north of Routes 25A and 54.

When winds are bad or frustration over access overwhelms you, why not fish the privacy of Long Island's overlooked north shore. I count no less than nine public boat-launching ramps scattered over the 40 approximate miles between Mattituck Inlet and Northport to the west. Using a keyed map, the way I did, locate the various launching ramps on the north shore for access. Inasmuch as local officials use your car to determine your presence, probably splitting fees with the tow truck operators, to keep you away from the exclusive local property, if you park at public launching ramps they have no way of knowing where you are and what you are doing. It could be risky to be sure, but you wouldn't be a surfcaster if you weren't accustomed to risk. The curse here is private property and the body of knowledge needed to deal with getting around that may be a bigger challenge than the fishing.

The outflows on Long Island's north shore do not serve large bays the way they do on the south and the big water in the back is the drive engine for any outflow. I think that any water movement, no matter how small, will draw gamefish. There are also some popular points spread along the north shore that produce because of their prominence on the shoreline.

Because I know little about this rather large and spread out collection of spots, and lack the specifics of each of them, I see more a collective value in their numbers and have rated them low for that reason. Still, the sense is there and the fishing is good for the right detective.

CONTACT TIP: A. P. White, Greenport, (631) 477-0008.

55
Sunken Meadow State Park
Long Island Sound
Kings Park, New York

BEST MONTHS TO FISH FOR STRIPERS: April to November.

RECOMMENDED METHODS: Lures and fly fishing.

FISH YOU CAN EXPECT TO CATCH: Stripers and blues.

HOW TO GET THERE: From the Long Island Expressway, take the Sunken Meadow State Parkway north to Kings Park and follow the state signs.

Sunken Meadow State Park is a natural because of the estuarine outflow that drains a tidal marsh and freshwater creek. Access is from the west side of the inlet opening, about ¼-mile walk from the parking lot. The park office issues night fishing permits for parking that are good for the season for $20.

There is a deep channel flanked by tidal flats that are wadable. The best opportunities are after dark in the late night when there is the least boat traffic. As with its other Long Island Sound counterpart in Connecticut, fish can be here all season. However, the summer southwest carries a lot of biting insects to this shore and the horseflies will accost you.

All access to Long Island's north shore is limited to another of those universal Striper Coast situations determined by discretion and commando tactics intended to defeat regional exclusivity. Area officials, influenced by local control, engage in controlling outsider access through the limiting of parking. Indeed tow operators in many communities split the towing fees with enforcement so there is every incentive for them to find your car, get it towed, and satisfy the complaints of local citizenry. For those reasons, we cannot in good conscience list the many productive outflows—east of Long Beach, Port Jefferson Harbor, Mattituck Inlet—all Long Island north shore spots that have promise. Because of the symbiotic relationship stripers have with outflows, they have to be good. Parking, access and discretion are outside the bounds of this book.

CONTACT TIP: Chester's, Farmingville, (631) 696-3800.

56
Long Island Power Authority Power Station (LILCO)
Northport, Long Island, New York

BEST MONTHS TO FISH FOR STRIPERS: February and March.

RECOMMENDED METHODS: Rubber shads and small bucktails fished deep in the outflow plume.

FISH YOU CAN EXPECT TO CATCH: Winter-over stripers up to 25 pounds max.

HOW TO GET THERE: Take Ocean Avenue to Eatons Road in Northport. (Tank farm on your left, west.) Approach from the east side of the intake channel. It is a half-mile walk.

On Long Island's north shore in Northport, a power station draws water from Aheroken Beach for the cooling of turbines. After the water has been used, it is released into a cooling lagoon before being spilled back into the Sound at adjacent Crab Meadow Beach. The action of the released water creates a waterfall at all but the highest of spring tides. Baitfish are attracted to this warmer outflow, and stripers collect there as a result. Sport fishing is concentrated at this waterfall, which has been in use for both cooling and angling for at least 40 years.

Striper populations from one season to another are variable probably due to outflow activity, which is dependent upon power plant use. Consequently, angling pressure there becomes a direct function of LIPA on-line needs. Recent years have shown robust mullet runs held by the warmer temperatures at the plume. Because of New York's striper season closure, this is all catch-and-release fishing. Since the rise in terrorism concerns, access to some power plant outflows has been restricted. However, the layout and proximity of the area being fished in proximity to sensitive properties has kept that from being a problem.

CONTACT TIP: J&J Sports, Patchogue, (631) 654-2311.

CONNECTICUT

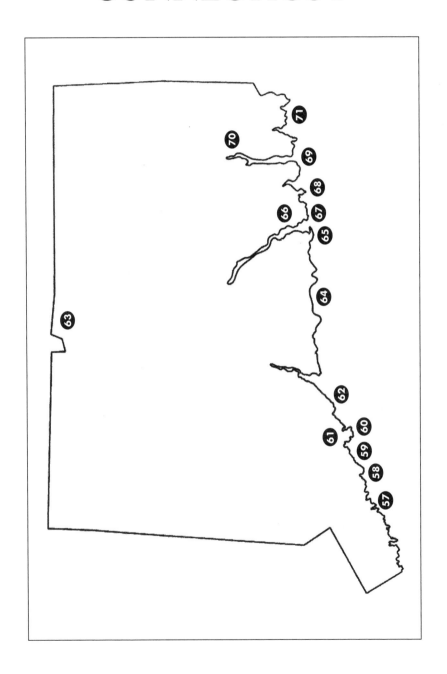

Connecticut

Private ownership of the shoreline reduces Connecticut's attractiveness as a shore fishing location much in the way that it has on the rest of the Striper Coast. Indeed, nearly all the spots listed here are within the bounds of state parks. No doubt there is excellent fishing in any number of other places, but local private control prevents access through a complicated variety of ordinances, selectively enforced parking regulations, and illegally hidden rights-of-way. Thus, and this is by no means unique to Connecticut, access opportunities are better for nearby residents, who enjoy circumvention and enforcement immunity. Usually, when our sweethearts wish us luck, they're referring to the fishing; for Connecticut they mean the parking.

Having said this, I am, nevertheless, pleased to report that the public property that emerges from my research is well chosen. A more dispassionate critic would probably regard the spots I've listed for Connecticut as exemplars of "multiple use," but I can't shake the feeling that they were either chosen by a fisherman or chosen with fishing uppermost in mind. We are compelled to applaud the idea that good fishing is no small criterion for the siting of state parks in this state. Modern policies, which will influence access in the future, favor a more reasonable balance in utilization of coastal resources. Today, waterfront sites have to provide meaningful public admittance, and the shore-bound angler can look forward to greater access opportunities as a result.

Unique to our treatment of Connecticut is the fact that government input was greater here than in any other state. First, Ron Rozsa, a biologist for Long Island Sound Programs and an enthusiastic shore fisherman as well as striperman, was able to help me during the preparation of the original years ago and directed me to an even better source in Rod Macleod, a biologist for Connecticut Marine Fisheries. With Macleod's input I had so many hot spots that the cuts list was nearly as long as the list of places I've described—not because Connecticut is superior, but because my information for this state was so complete and derived in such measure from professional sources. It's what these guys do.

Another anomaly that I bumped into, much to my delight, is that this state is awash with saltwater fly fishers. Thus, while it is not necessarily the case, the notion that Connecticut's fly fishing is better than elsewhere emerges here, more as a result of local insistence than natural conditions.

What fun fishing you could have going to the places that have failed to make the cut. I commend the following to your indulgence with the reminder that all the judgments in this book are ultimately subjective:

Greenwich Point Park, Stamford
Shippan Point, Stamford
Sherwood Island State Park, Westport
Pleasure Beach/Town Pier, Bridgeport
Long Beach, Stratford/Bridgeport
Stratford Point, Stratford
Power plant on the Housatonic, Devon
Milford Harbor East and West Jetties
Sandy Point, West Haven
Noank Town Dock
Rocky Neck State Park, Old Lyme
Black Hall River Bridge

57

Calf Pasture Point and Town Pier
South Norwalk, Connecticut

BEST MONTHS TO FISH: March through June, and September through November.

RECOMMENDED METHODS: Chunks, plugs, fly fishing, and sea worms.

FISH YOU CAN EXPECT TO CATCH: Stripers, bluefish, and some blackfish.

HOW TO GET THERE: Take exit 16 off I–95 and turn left at the traffic light onto East Avenue. Follow East Avenue to a traffic circle, then bear right onto Gregory Boulevard. Take a right onto Ludlow Parkway and follow it to its end.

People who fish the town pier like to use cut bait (chunks) of menhaden, herring, or mackerel held on the bottom with a sinker. The popularity of this spot would preclude any opportunity for lure fishing during all but the deepest hours of the night. The best tide phase at this spot is high water, when it is not possible to fish the bar out front. The pier is also popular in September for snapper blues when they are at a point in their development of inch-per-week growth. Look for some decent winter flounder fishing in March with sea worms. There is some blackfish fishing, but that is not what has made this spot.

On the bar out front, the gang enjoys plugging swimmers like Rebels, Mambo Minnows, and Red Fins tied direct. Wading is not possible until the tide is down to around halfway. If the fishing proves to be any good, regulars will stay until rising water forces them off; the drop, because of combining currents of the Norwalk River, has an edge. Protected by the Norwalk Islands, the bar is popular with fly fishermen. As with the pier, if there is room and water is low enough for a sand spike, some people will chunk from the bar.

John Baldino, fishing from a boat in the Norwalk Islands right off Calf Pasture Point, landed a 71-pound striper only a few years ago. This proves that the big mamas can be there. During daylight, a town parking permit is required between Memorial Day and Labor Day, but fishing is open to anyone after closing time. There are fewer hassles in spring and fall.

CONTACT TIP: Fisherman's World, East Norwalk, (203) 866-1075.

58
Cedar Point and Compo Beach
Westport, Connecticut

BEST MONTHS TO FISH: March through June, and September through November.

RECOMMENDED METHODS: Swimming plugs, cut baits, sea worms, and fly fishing.

FISH YOU CAN EXPECT TO CATCH: Stripers and bluefish.

HOW TO GET THERE: From exit 18 off I–95, get onto the Sherwood Island State Park Connector northbound, then take a left (west) onto Green Farms Road. A left onto Hills Point Road

Blues can be found around the river mouth.

leads to the beach. Take a right (south) onto Compo Road, then take the next left for the entrance.

These two spots are combined because they are adjacent and fished as well as spoken of by locals in the same breath. Cedar Point is a little more protected at the river mouth, while Compo Beach is more open to the Sound. Opportunities here reflect those at Calf Point. Differences often develop around the type and location of baitfish that have drawn gamefish here in the first place. It is a case of who has the bait where the bunker happen to be. Naturally, the influence of the Saugatuck River at the west end (Cedar Point) holds an edge for the dropping tide, but the open water and stony shore of Slates, on the east end of Compo, more than compensate for that.

155

Depending on the winds the fly fishers prefer the river mouth, even more so if the tide is dropping. There is enough space here for you to fish bait or plug, with some anglers doing both—plugging with their eye on a baited rod. At the west end of Compo Beach, in front of the cannons, there is a serious blackfish run spring and fall. Tackle shops say to block out early May and late October on your calendar.

As at Calf Pasture, summer hassles and parking stickers are the rule, but the best fishing is at the two quiet ends of the season. While there may not be any 70-pounders on the record books for this hot spot, all agree it rates one better than Calf Pasture.

CONTACT TIP: Call the Sportsman's Den, Cos Cob, (203) 869-3234.

59
Penfield Reef
Fairfield, Connecticut

BEST MONTHS TO FISH: May through November.

RECOMMENDED METHODS: Fly fishing and swimming plugs.

FISH YOU CAN EXPECT TO CATCH: Stripers and bluefish.

HOW TO GET THERE: Take exit 22 from I–95 to Round Hill Road to Route 1; then take a right. At the traffic light, take a left onto Reef Road, which leads to the Sound. Parking is available at a recreation park on the left side. Across the road, on the left, about 50 yards past the stop sign, there is a walkway between two houses, which, after ¼ mile, leads to a beach walkway.

Penfield Reef is a rock-and-cobble sand spit that extends into Long Island Sound for about a mile. During low tide, the spit is exposed enough for fishermen in waders to follow it down. Thus, this place is popular during a falling tide. One of the few spots where fly fishing leads the way, it remains a good place for plug fishermen who utilize swimming plugs during the night.

Of course, the aforementioned rules are not hard and fast. Cut baits can be used—tackle shops say that live eels are becoming increasingly popular, and no doubt there are other species available at selected locations. Those who know their way around here in the dark of night do use the flood tide to their advantage, but, until you know the ropes, I would not advise you to chance getting confused in a rising tide and getting trapped in deep water.

CONTACT TIP: Call Ted's Bait and Tackle, Bridgeport, (203) 366-7615.

60
Saint Mary's Beach, Ash Creek, and Henry J. Moore Fishing Pier
Fairfield, Connecticut

BEST MONTHS TO FISH: April through November.

RECOMMENDED METHODS: Cut bait (menhaden, herring, or mackerel) and swimming plugs.

FISH YOU CAN EXPECT TO CATCH: Stripers, bluefish, blackfish, and fluke.

HOW TO GET THERE: Ash Creek and the Moore Fishing Pier are at the South Benson Marina. From I–95 take exit 23 to Route 1 south. Take a left (after McDonald's) onto South Benson Road, then a left onto Oil Field Road, then a right onto Turney Road to the marina. For Saint Mary's Beach, take exit 25 off I–95 onto Fairfield Avenue south. Take a left at Gillman Street and continue to the east side of Ash Creek. Parking and access are provided.

Saint Mary's Beach faces the open Long Island Sound where the bottom is composed of boulders and rocks. Across from the beach is the Henry J. Moore Fishing Pier, which is actually an extension of a rip-rap embankment bordering Ash Creek Channel. The channel is popular with stripermen who watch the creek at night for feeding linesides that gorge on bait there, particularly during a falling tide.

Menhaden schools frequent Ash Creek and are often trapped in the marina basin by predators. Blues exhibit the same behavior as stripers but are more likely than stripers to do so in daylight. For day anglers, there is a good fluke run in the channel out front during the late summer and early fall. The rocky bottom of Saint Mary's appeals to blackfish in spring, when their spawning run is on. Look for them the third week in April and use sea worms. Many wanted to rate this spot a three for stripers—a tough call.

CONTACT TIP: Ted's, Bridgeport, (203) 366-7615.

The "Housie" is a river system with everything, including stripers.

61
Housatonic River
Stratford, Connecticut

BEST MONTHS TO FISH: April, May, October, November.

RECOMMENDED METHODS: Plugs and fly fishing.

FISH YOU CAN EXPECT TO CATCH: Stripers and blues, plus a mixed bag, including freshwater species, upriver.

HOW TO GET THERE: From Route 95 take exit 34 south for ¹⁄₁₀ of a mile then go right onto Bridgeport Avenue; ½ mile later go left onto Naugatuck Avenue. Next drive ½ mile to a right on

Milford Point Road. It is a mile to Laurel Beach, and from there you can follow the shore southwest until you reach the Audubon gate.

The Housatonic River is another of those environmental success stories underlined by both cleaner water and effective fisheries management. The spot's coverage here is really a river system, which zeros in on two locations: the mouth of the "Housey" at Milford Point in Stratford on the river's east bank; and, the first upstream dam in Darby, which marks the end of tidewater and stops fish from any further upstream migration. The Milford Point location is the most important as it relates to saltwater striper fishing.

Here, at the mouth of the river, strong tidal currents sweep past Milford Point. On the dropping tide the 750-acre tidal marsh of Nells Island, with its numerous salt creeks, keeps a steady dole of estuarine baitfish sweeping past the point. The island itself is state property operated as the Charles E. Wheeler Wildlife Management Area. The last mile of Long Island Sound beachfront is managed by the Milford branch of the Connecticut Audubon Society, which allows night fishing along with a key to their locked gate. Locals acquire memberships and keys by joining the Audubon. It is the only way to deal with the stringent parking maintained by local restrictions. Even when accessed properly, it is still a 20-minute walk to the good fishing.

Two spots dominate this location: Milford Point itself, which is most seaward; and, the spur about 1,000 feet northwest, upriver, facing the swampy island. Both tides are good, but I give the drop an edge. Everybody either plugs or fly fishes here after dark.

DARBY DAM

Another local aspect of the Housatonic River is to fish at the Dam in Darby where there is public parking. However, that far upstream the entire character, while it is still brackish, changes to a mixed bag of both fresh- and saltwater species. Season depending, the hot periods are spring and fall for stripers up to 30 pounds, with an iffy winter-over fishery. Under the dam they get largemouth bass, white and yellow perch, sea-run trout that apparently washed down from a robust catch-and-release management upriver and even an occasional Atlantic salmon. When fishing is good, there can be some pretty wild collections of anglers that—depending upon your attitude—qualify as group sport. A freshwater fishing license is needed north or upstream of the Wilbur Cross/Merritt Parkway (Route 15).

We rate this hot spot as a one star because of the access limitations and hassle related to Audubon memberships. All the same, the fishing is considerably better than that or it would not be in this book.

CONTACT TIP: Call Stratford Bait and Tackle, Stratford, (203) 377-8091.

62

Silver Sands State Park (Charles Island)
Milford, Connecticut

BEST MONTHS TO FISH: May through November.
RECOMMENDED METHODS: Fly fishing, swimming plugs, and cut baits.

FISH YOU CAN EXPECT TO CATCH: Stripers and bluefish.

HOW TO GET THERE: From I–95, take exit 35, Schoolhouse Road south. Turn right onto Route 1 (Bridgeport Avenue), then left onto Meadows End Road. Follow Meadows End straight onto Pumpkin Delight Road. At the end of this road, turn right onto Monroe Street, then left onto Nettleton. Turn left at the barricade onto the Park Service road and follow it to the end. (Access will be changing, as this park is presently under development, and it is still is unclear how roads will be managed.)

The major attraction of this hot spot is a ½-mile bar that connects with Charles Island. Wader-clad regulars like to work the rips that form between the island and shore, but access to the island is only possible at low tide, and it is necessary for anyone who goes there to keep in mind the potential for being trapped. Because surf fishing is best done at night, it is mandatory that anyone doing any wading here be certain about tide, visibility, and direction. Until you are completely familiar with the area, be especially cautious.

No doubt other species can be taken here, but the targets are stripers and blues, and artificials dominate the methods. Silver Sands is not for everyone. On the other hand, if you know the striper ropes, this is a place worthy of finely tuned attentions. Swimming plugs tied direct—not encumbered with a wire leader—work well on slurping stripers. Fly fishermen should plan to use floating lines and the usual streamer patterns. Good spot.

CONTACT TIP: Stratford Bait and Tackle, Stratford, (203) 377-8091.

63
Enfield Dam
Connecticut River
Suffield, Connecticut

BEST MONTHS TO FISH: Late April to late June.
RECOMMENDED METHODS: Alewife baits and big swimming plugs.
FISH YOU CAN EXPECT TO CATCH: Stripers and shad.
HOW TO GET THERE: From I–91 take exit 47B to Route 190 west. After crossing the river, take Route 159 south, then take the first left onto Canal Street.

Another herring-run fishery that is highly seasonal, Enfield Dam reflects population trends of both indigenous bait and stripers. Each spring linesides follow alewives and white shad up from the Sound to the eroding dam where both mill about. Without bait there are no stripers.

While anglers line up on both banks to toss baits and plugs, the west bank has the edge because of two nearby holes, better flow characteristics, and the availability of parking at Old Canal Park. Dependent upon snowmelt, spring water levels can be highly variable: one day fishermen can wade far out into the river among the rocks; another day the river roars white, nearly burying the dam. With such conditions, there is some hazard to the river. Drownings take place every year, for example, although most victims are from boats. While examining conditions, it is good to keep in mind that water temperatures, which trigger the runs of both bait and gamefish, are more suitable when the water is low because snowmelt is colder. Otherwise, the later in the season, the better and bigger the bass run. As with the rest of the Striper Coast, small fish arrive first, in April, and the cows become numerous in late May. Look for a top fish in the low forties and a predominance of smaller linesides. Naturally, the river will mirror coastwide population trends.

You may have to fish heavy tackle in order to deal with the current and crowds. Locals can often be seen carrying two rods—a light 6-footer for snagging baits and a meat stick for the actual fishing. Here, a freshwater fishing license is required despite its tidewater status. Keep in mind that the use of herring as bait is not legal as the herring in all of Southern New England are now protected to restore the once robust runs.

CONTACT TIP: Connecticut Outfitters, Hartford, (860) 296-0110.

64
Hammonasset Beach State Park
Madison, Connecticut

BEST MONTHS TO FISH: May through November.
RECOMMENDED METHODS: Sea worms, chunks (bunker and mackerel), live eels, poppers, and swimmers.
FISH YOU CAN EXPECT TO CATCH: Stripers and bluefish.
HOW TO GET THERE: From I–95 take exit 62, then follow the signs to the park.

The rock jetty at Meigs Point attracts the majority of angling attention within Hammonasset Beach State Park. Bottom fishermen tend to gather here in large crowds during seasonal peaks and weekends. (Fishing is limited to the jetty during the summer season.) The waters at the very end of the jetty are most popular because of the depth there. By fall—particularly after dark, which is a time when the best fishing of the year is available—this spot is pure solitude. The entire beach is open after Labor Day, and it is not uncommon for great schools of bluefish to be seen within casting distance. Park personnel issue permits for fishing after closing time so that anglers can drive their cars from the entrance gate to the beach.

Madison's Stu Jones, winner of the 1994 Massachusetts Governor's Cup with a 57-pounder, likes Meigs Point. "I like the flood better than the ebb here because of how the rip makes up with the jetty," said Jones. "During falling water your eel or plug has to go through rocks that are fouled with old tackle and lines that are caught there. But, during the rise, the current flow is northwest and the rip line sets up right at your feet. I flip eels underhand back at the submerged rocks, drifting them through the rip like garden worms for trout. I have been pretty successful."

CONTACT TIP: Antlers and Anglers, Madison, (860) 245-1007.

65
Cornfield Point
Old Saybrook, Connecticut

BEST MONTHS TO FISH: May through November (but skip August).
RECOMMENDED METHODS: Plugs, eels, fly fishing, chunks, and crabs.

Big swimming plugs are popular here.

FISH YOU CAN EXPECT TO CATCH: Stripers, bluefish, and blackfish.

HOW TO GET THERE: From I–95 take exit 67 onto Route 1 south, then take a left at the light onto Route 154 south, follow to a left turn onto Cornfield Point Road, and continue to land's end.

All of this rocky shoreline is productive, but the fishing improves as one makes one's way west to the point. Watch for evidence of moving water, which is more likely down to the right. Big swimming plugs are popular here as are live eels, but because of the rocks, eel retrieve speeds should be slightly faster to keep them from getting lost. Fly fishers like the sand flats to the north. You can also access these flats from the Old Saybrook Town Beach, although public access is often restricted in the summer.

As in any other southwest-facing location, winds from that quarter improve things; however, a strong southeaster, usually an indication of an impending storm, also makes the interaction of the currents better. Starting in early October, there is a great fall run of good-sized blackfish that take green or hermit crabs like candy.

This is a popular local spot with fragile access considerations. Some anglers park at the rear of the Castle Inn lot, but officials tell me that it is illegal to do so and that your car may be towed. Yes, parking is a problem.

CONTACT TIP: River's End Tackle, Old Saybrook, (860) 388-2283.

66
Connecticut Department of Environmental Protection Marine Headquarters
Old Lyme, Connecticut

BEST MONTHS TO FISH: March through December.

RECOMMENDED METHODS: Baits or lures, depending on the species, and fly fishing.

FISH YOU CAN EXPECT TO CATCH: Stripers, bluefish, and blackfish.

HOW TO GET THERE: Take exit 70 from I–95 to Route 156 north; then take a right onto Ferry Road and continue to land's end. There will be signs.

A fishing pier, completed in the spring of '93, extends from the south end of the state property (beneath the Old Lyme railroad bridge) to the mouth of the Lieutenant River—a fly-fishing mecca. This one earns hot-spot status because it is highly accessible and productive on account of its placement on the Connecticut River—hardly a risky call. Open twenty-four hours a day, it is intended to be the answer to the problems that so often bedevil shore fishing. Fly fishers leave the end of the pier and wade the bars in the deep night with floating lines. Patterns are dressed to imitate river shiners, sperling and—some years—baby bunker.

CONTACT TIP: River's End Tackle, Old Saybrook, (860) 388-2283.

67
Sound View Beach
Old Lyme, Connecticut

BEST MONTHS TO FISH: May, June, October, and November.

RECOMMENDED METHODS: Plugs, live or rigged eels, and fly fishing.

FISH YOU CAN EXPECT TO CATCH: Stripers and blues.

HOW TO GET THERE: From I–95 take exit 71 onto Four Mile River Road. Take a right on Route 156 at the stop sign, then a left onto Hartford Avenue and follow to the end. Parking is limited and at your own risk.

Two major areas of structure on this sandy, gently sloping beach should be tested first. About 300 yards west of the parking lot, there is a small rocky point that is popular two hours either side of high tide. Outside those hours, efforts should be cursory, and I'm told that the sand before that is a waste of time.

The other spot, Griswold Point, is about a mile west and just about as far as many of us are willing to walk. Matt Zajac, a competent river guide and regular, however, tells me that it is Connecticut's answer to the Cape's old-time Chatham Inlet, only smaller—and well worth the effort. The reason for this is that currents from the Blackhall and Connecticut Rivers collide with Long Island Sound to create a garland of moving water, bait, stripers, and blues. Here, juvenile herring and menhaden emigrate from the nearby Connecticut River in late summer and fall (mature spawning baitfish earlier). Onshore sou'west winds stir it up for better fishing, and nor'westers cause the Connecticut River water to move better. Casting from shore, you can reach a depth of 13 feet. There is excellent fishing all through the dropping tide here, so try it after having worked the rocky outcropping mentioned earlier at high tide. While all methods work, this is dreamland for fly fishers. Possibly the best-in-state!

CONTACT TIP: River's End Tackle, Old Saybrook, (860) 388-2283.

68
Niantic River
Niantic, Connecticut

BEST MONTHS TO FISH: May through November.

RECOMMENDED METHODS: Bunkers, herring, bucktail jigs, live eels, and fly fishing.

FISH YOU CAN EXPECT TO CATCH: Stripers and bluefish.

HOW TO GET THERE: For the western shore, take exit 74 from I–95 to Route 161 toward Niantic, then make a left at the light onto Route 156. Either take the left road before the Niantic River Drawbridge and follow to the end, or take a left immediately after the drawbridge, then a left at the stop sign. Safe parking on the west, or Niantic, side of the river is limited to the access ramp on the north side of the road. Eastern shore access is from Route 156, Rope Ferry Road. At the traffic light, turn north onto Niantic River Road, take the first left onto B Street, turn left onto Fourth Street, and take the first right onto Rope Ferry Road to public parking at the end.

Fishing is done from the railroad bridge at the mouth of the Niantic River. To the south, or seaward of the railroad track, you can fish both sides of the river. There is also good fishing on the west bank between the bridges. Beaches on both sides of the river mouth produce good fishing, with the eastern shore having an edge.

When there are bunker in the river—and thus the opportunity to snag fresh baits—it is possible to feed one from this bridge and do very well with both stripers and blues. At times, there have been some moby blues taken here in this way. Currents from this river bridge are too powerful for bottom fishing, and plugging, except at slack tide, is not a viable alternative. Nevertheless, a bucktail jig, for those who use them well and allow them to drift deep, can be used for stripers in the night if there are no fresh baits available. The best water is during the drop in tide.

Pat Abate, a local regular with a coastwide reputation, told me that about twenty years ago there was a striper taken here that weighed in the mid-sixties. Not too shabby. Eddies or slack tides in which you can hold bottom produce some decent blackfish. It is possible to fish bottom on the south side of the inlet. Also, some surfcasters like to fish live eels by casting and retrieving slowly.

Just about any bait found coastwide is represented here and thus can be used with delivery methods dictated by the motion of the water. Anglers have been known to lament the oft-repeated complaint that bass will show up in the Niantic—usually in the deep of night—slashing and slurping but not taking any baits or artificials. Abate says that this happens when the squid are abundant, but it may also occur during June worm hatches, which have driven otherwise calm people stark raving mad. South of the inlet, particularly on the outgoing tide, when bait is being swept past, the action can be better than in the inlet. That is one reason why it is a popular fly-fishing spot.

CONTACT TIP: Hillyers Tackle Shop, Waterford, (860) 443-7615.

69
Harkness Memorial State Park
Waterford, Connecticut

BEST MONTHS TO FISH: May through November, although August is slow.

RECOMMENDED METHODS: Plugs, cut baits, eels, hermit crabs, and fly fishing.

FISH YOU CAN EXPECT TO CATCH: Stripers, bluefish, blackfish, and some fluke.

HOW TO GET THERE: From I–95, take exit 75 onto Route 1 east and drive four miles to a right turn.

The best fishing is west (to the right) of this rocky, curving shoreline. The boulder-strewn shore offers plenty of attractive hiding places for good-sized stripers. There is also a reef within casting distance that has to draw some linesides to the area.

Some Harkness regulars will come equipped to fish cut bait (menhaden or mackerel) but have a supply of plugs in the bag—swimmers at night and poppers by day—for when they see or hear fish working. Of course, when things are known to be good, surf fishers arrive with live eels. While stripers are what most are seeking, bluefish often end up as targets of opportunity. With all the rocks, this is also a great blackfish spot starting in early October. Use green or hermit crabs with a bank sinker on the bottom. The sandy shallow areas near Goshen Cove are popular with fly fishers who use floating lines.

The best fishing time for all methods is two hours either side of high tide, particularly when this period matches up with dawn or dusk. No parking hassles.

CONTACT TIP: River's End Tackle, (860) 388-2283.

70

Thames River
Norwich, Connecticut

BEST MONTHS TO FISH FOR STRIPERS: November through March.

RECOMMENDED METHODS: Small lures like jigs and Super Fluke, some bottom baits.

FISH YOU CAN EXPECT TO CATCH: Winter-over stripers, blues in the summer.

HOW TO GET THERE: This is more a region than a particular spot. From Route 395 take exit 80 east into Norwich.

The qualifying aspect of the Thames River for this book is that it is one of those rare winter-over fisheries not all that common on the Striper Coast. A moderate migratory population of stripers returns to the Norwich area every winter providing angling opportunity for boat and shore fishermen. No one knows why this winter fishery has evolved because the warm-water discharge once believed to draw winter fish has become less dependable with the decommissioning of the old Montville Power Plant that once reliably produced a robust warm-water discharge. There is a new power plant but, surprisingly, the fishing does not always take place right at the occasional warm-water outflow. The conditions producing the best fishing remain sort of a mystery, where it is no longer as simple as finding the plant in power production by watching the steam and smoke from its stacks. At times the west bank of the Thames downstream and south of the plant is a suitable shore fishing location, but the stripers are often on the move even when water is mid-winter cold.

Just as many shore fish are taken from the Norwich docks right in town. While this upstream location remains tidal, there is less reliance on tide in this fishery than might be found elsewhere. There has been considerable loss of access to the river over the years, but state-owned and -managed Fort Shantock State Park in Montville (off Route 32 north of the Pequot Bridge) is open for fishing and located in the prime parts of the river. The Norwich Marina and dock right in Norwich are commonly bait fished on the bottom. The time was when fresh herring or alewives were the ticket, but recent restrictions on their use to protect these baitfish have banned that. If alewife populations ever recover, they could again be a viable bait choice.

Use of artificials works best if on the small side and running deep, as stripers tend to stack on the bottom. Forget poppers. The old-time MirrOLures your uncle used have largely been replaced with the plethora of modern deep-running rubber shads. Super Flukes were in the limelight at the time of this writing but, fishing being what it is, that could change quickly. It is safe to say that whatever works elsewhere will have its day on the Thames. Drastic changes in temperatures are thought to enhance the fishing.

The best lineside you'll ever see here would not weigh over 30 pounds with the average more like five pounds. There was a 57-pounder taken in the region years ago but I wouldn't count on that happening again. Heavy breathers of the Striper Coast lust over this spot more because of the off-season opportunity it provides as a winter fishery. Notwithstanding, that might just be the injustice in the reputation of the place. Spring runs of alewives, with their striper-drawing scent, provide a great spring run of new fish after winter-overs have left sustaining activity well into

June. Anglers gather at the Shetucket River Dam in spring to cash in on new fish drawn upriver by the alewife run. There is also a lot of activity behind the football field on the Shetucket's east bank along Route 165 more because of public access. November stripers pour in while suitable water temperatures encourage their feeding. Schools of bunker, vast many summer seasons, will draw bluefish during what some might call the "off months."

Gales Ferry (take Route 12 to Stoddard Wharf Road), according to the Division of Marine Fisheries, is a famous summer hot spot for both bass and blues. The river makes a bend here and the main channel comes within casting range of the riverbank. Menhaden are the forage base that are chunked on the bottom, but the gang uses swimmers and poppers during this warm-weather fishing period.

A freshwater fishing license is required for the whole area in spite of there being so much salt in the grog. Connecticut policy for setting the line for license requirement varies from river to river. We've found it necessary to lower the rating of this hot spot due to reduced access, and a reputation for boat fishing that is greater than that from the shore.

CONTACT TIP: Fish Connection, Preston, (860) 885-1739.

71
Bluff Point State Park
Groton, Connecticut

BEST MONTHS TO FISH: April through November.
RECOMMENDED METHODS: Plugs or baits, depending on the species.

FISH YOU CAN EXPECT TO CATCH: Stripers, bluefish, blackfish, scup, and winter flounder.

HOW TO GET THERE: Take exit 88 from I–95 to Route 117 south. Take a right on Route 1, then a left at the traffic light onto Depot Road and follow it to the end under the railroad tracks and into the park.

The rocky shoreline at Bluff Point is about ¾ mile from the parking lot. Striperwise, things don't get going here until June, but they hold well into November. Expect blues from July into November. All the methods—cut baits and plugs—that work elsewhere are utilized here. Among the rockier areas, anticipate some blackfish (tautog) in late April. The best bait at that time of year is a sea worm on the bottom with a bank sinker. For scup (porgies), fish the sandy areas with freshwater-sized light tackle using a fingernail-sized sliver of squid or a small section of broken sea worm with a trout hook. The first scup appear in June, and they become more numerous as summer goes on.

Poquonock Cove, which is off to the west in the park, and closer, is a good spot for winter flounder in early spring on the flood tide. Use sea worms and small hooks.

CONTACT TIP: Shaffer's Boat Livery, Mystic, (860) 536-8713.

INLETS: WHERE STRIPERS PROWL

One of the biggest issues in working the striper surf is knowing how to look for them without covering the entire coast. It is necessary to know the kind of water where stripers are likely to appear. First, they like moving water because they can breathe more easily; secondly, they can hold in currents for passing bait, enhancing their foraging opportunities. That kind of water can be found at narrows and points that obstruct the passage of the tides. However, one's best chance of locating robust currents is in the outflow of an inlet, a place where a coastal bay or salt pond fills or empties into the open ocean.

The hydrology of inlets and outflows needs a lot of understanding because of the complexity of the two containers—the open ocean and the coastal pond, river mouth, or bay. It is never enough to trust a tide chart for the timing of the tidal flow because a number of variables come into play that determine when the water will actually change direction. Many surfmen are bewildered by the differences in water movement. They go to an outflow at high tide and when they get there water is pouring in as though the tide was still rising. What is happening is that the larger open ocean, which has reached high tide, has not yet filled the smaller container—the estuary. The tide will not slack until the two spaces—ocean and pond—have a common level. Similarly, at low tide in the front, water will continue to fall from the back pond even when the front has begun to rise and, again, slack low will not occur until the two are level. Various inlets have different lag times—when the two levels are equal—and you need to become familiar with the ones you frequent. Because of the currents incidental to this tidal activity, it is an easier place for all gamefish to feed.

Most gamefish, not only stripers, will take advantage of this moving water for feeding. Just about any species one can think of can be found in outflows waiting for the natural handout that occurs from the estuaries. I have known cod, pollack, bonito, and bluefish to hold in the currents which they probably find through a combination of the scent of bait and differences in water temperature caused by the sun's warming of the smaller back ponds, which can be more subject to these influences with its lower volume.

All species of trout and salmon in fresh water utilize the currents that flow into and even out of lakes and ponds. Like ocean species, these fish will move up into the currents of a feeder stream holding in places where they can stay in position with little effort while enjoying the advantages hard-moving water provides. Back to salt water.

Inlet structure can vary. While jetties flank some outflows, others are bordered and interspersed with sandbars. These can shift and change, adding a measure of hazard to walking around in strange places after dark. It is easy on some outflow distant from the dry beach to become so absorbed with the fishing and the assurance of falling water as to overlook that the tide in the front has begun to rise while the water in back is still flowing out. Places where the tidal exchange is greater, the effect upon the danger is even greater. It is here that lag will get you. And going back to shore over or at the top of your waders will make you wish you had paid closer attention to the tide. It's embarrassing to be puffing up your rubber ducky to get back to your buggy.

Timing is everything in inlet fishing. That is why it is so important to understand the tidal lag of any location that fills and empties along the coast. The most popular tide choice is to fish an outflow during a dropping tide, because gamefish, and stripers are the most likely, will hold in the current for that natural handout. Depending upon the intensity of the current, and the depth of the channel created by the robust currents that are certain to be there, effective fishing depends upon one's ability to penetrate the water column if the water is deep and on the quality of the presentation if the water is shallow. In my opinion, the drop is best.

The longer the tide falls, the more time the situation has had to lure fish to the opening. Thus, I would always make a point of timing my night, taking lag into account, so as to be there during the tail end of the drop while it is still dark. Also, remember you heard it here, when the inlet currents are slacking, everything that was in front that could not be reached by all those gorillas you were fishing with is about to change positions. In many popular hot spots gamefish that were too far, too deep, or too selective are changing positions when the tide is slacking low. It is never a good idea to rest or eat your lunch when the water is slowing for that reason. The musical chairs playing out in front of you are also enhanced by the reduction in water volume that still entertains the same number of gamefish. Where you started fishing in 10 feet of water, the same number of stripers is now holding in five. It is a good time.

The same outflows that pulled fish up from the ocean will pull fish up from the back pond or estuary during the rise. Never think that stripers are reluctant to run narrow and shallow openings, because these are anadromous species that were born in the shallows of freshwater rivers. Commonly, the fishing is as good during a rise in tide as it was for the drop. Even so, this tide is less popular and gets much less attention from the angling public, so it is possible to fish by yourself on the incoming when there was no place to park during the drop in tide. In addition, the timing is sometimes interfered with by daylight or boat traffic—no small consideration in many places.

The tidal reversal promotes a transposition in where to fish. Just as the crowd gathered as far out as they could for the seaward dropping tide, it becomes necessary to gather in the back where the water fills the bay or pond. It is really the same thing, only the volume of water is increasing. On the other hand, in the back there are fewer people with whom to share the fish and fishing.

The places that taught me the importance of inlets were in Rhode Island flanked by jetties. I have seen and used both extremes that supported the notion of outflow fishing. When you fish the jetty at Barnegat, moving water flows east, pulling fish up from the open Atlantic; and when you are at its west end in the back, the currents toll stripers up from the bay during a rise in tide. While serving as an extreme example of an inlet, even Montauk guards the entrance to Long Island Sound. Furthermore, I would never overlook a small ankle-deep creek running into the ocean. They all lure gamefish.

When I researched my original *Striper Hot Spots,* the first edition that cataloged the best surfcasting locations on the Striper Coast, I found that ⅔ of the widely held best places to fish were inlets, a result that manifests itself in this edition as well. For a person interested in the best fishing, it is kind of a no-brainer to find these outflows

No precept on proper surfcasting can be overlooked even in inlet fishing, so it is important to remember the other things. You are still expected to fish at night if you want results—and, you can have good night fishing that extends into the dawn. Crowds are more likely in these places, thus cooperation with other anglers, often with rotation where casting is done in turn, is mandatory or it is not fun nor productive. Method choices have to be in harmony so that all are fishing the same way. You can't have five people drifting plugs while another anchors bait on the bottom.

Estuaries, rivers, and bays provide safe harbor for mooring boats; a consequence of that is that there is close in boat traffic that interrupts fishing. Even though boats will move holding gamefish from their lies in the current, the fish will come back. Fighting fish with boats plying the inlet can cause an angler to be cut off. Thus, cooperation has to be as directed to passing boats as it is to the guys on your jetty or bar. Each outflow is different and each of them offers variable levels of opportunity. Still, if I had nothing else to go by, I would start where rivers meet the sea. Working the spots where a dropping tide pulls stripers from deep water is your best bet.

PICK OF THE MONTH

Here is a calendar of hot spots:

February: Thames River, Connecticut (number 70)
March: Troy Dam, Hudson River (number 41)
April: Lower Delaware River (number 13)
May: Upper Delaware River (number 15)
June: Enfield Dam, Connecticut (number 63)
July*: Orient Point (number 53)
August*: Niantic River (number 68)
September*: Sandy Hook Point (number 37)
October: Montauk Point (number 52)
November: Island Beach State Park, New Jersey (number 31)
December: Cape Point, Buxton, North Carolina (number 3)

*These are not productive months for striper fishing in the Middle Atlantic states of the Striper Coast. Selections during summer are sort of make-do to fill the calender. We suggest that these months would be best spent in New England, east of those locations treated here. For a similar compendium of hot spots, see *Striper Hot Spots—New England*.

BEST IN SPECIES

Here is a list of locations that are best for each of the following commonly sought species:

Striped bass: Montauk Point (number 52)
Bluefish: Island Beach State Park (number 31)
Red drum: Cape Point at Buxton (number 3)
Weakfish: Moriches Inlet (number 49)
Cobia: Outer Banks Fishing Piers (number 6)
Summer flounder (fluke): Barnegat Inlet North Jetty (number 29)
American white shad: Troy Dam, Hudson River (number 41)
Blackfish (tautog): Orient Point (number 53)
Croaker: Pamlico Sound Shallows (number 5)
Kingfish: Delaware State Parks (number 12)

USUAL AND CUSTOMARY REQUIREMENTS FOR AN OVER-SAND VEHICLE

The following items and accepted modes of behavior are usual for acquisition of permits to drive over sand. These requirements—sizes, strengths, and ratings—vary from one jurisdiction to another and are intended only to be representative of what is needed for a beach permit.

- Shovel (heavy-duty military or entrenching)
- Tow rope or chain
- Jack and support stand
- Street-legal tires (snow or mud tread often rejected)
- Spare tire
- Low-pressure tire gauge (0–20 lbs.)
- First-aid kit (Coast Guard approved)
- Fire extinguisher (CG or ICC approved)
- Road flares
- Flashlight
- Auto insurance
- Four-wheel drive

All driving must be on prescribed dune trails or on the front beach.

Avoid bathing areas and other examples of user conflict.

Stay out of the dunes or any areas where vegetation might be compromised.

Observe speed limits on beaches, which vary from 5 to 15 miles per hour.

Ruts or holes caused by stuck vehicles must be filled and any debris removed.

Do not allow outside passengers (usually in the form of tailgate sitters).

Headlights must be used at all times.

Keep off of bird nesting areas and stay out of marked areas.

There is a trend in some jurisdictions to recognize the importance of vehicle under-carriage clearance on sport utility vehicles prior to the granting of beach permits. The apparent reason for this is that automakers have become conscious of rollover statistics and have sought to lower centers of gravity at the expense of off-road performance. Inasmuch as so many of today's SUVs have little off-road use, the trend toward better highway performance with so little regard for clearance has made it necessary for these jurisdictions to define the limits of allowable space between the beach and the vehicle's underside—seven inches in one case. It is a good rule, but its importance is that this additional regulation is likely to spread among the various beaches where over-sand vehicles are allowed. For both permit and performance you need to be conscious of this clearance in your selection of off-road vehicle for beach use because clearance is critical to better over-sand performance.